D1251701

THE LOST BOOK OF
ALEXANDER
THE GREAT

THE LOST BOOK OF
ALEXANDER
THE GREAT

Andrew Young

WESTHOLME

Yardley

Frontispiece: A late 2nd century B.C. mosaic depicting Alexander confronting Darius at the Battle of Issus, 333 B.C. (*Museo Nazionale, Naples, Italy*)

©2014 Andrew Young
Maps by Paul Dangel
Maps ©2014 Westholme Publishing

Westholme Publishing, LLC
904 Edgewood Road
Yardley, Pennsylvania 19067
Visit our Web site at www.westholmepublishing.com

First Printing May 2014
10 9 8 7 6 5 4 3 2 1
ISBN: 978-1-59416-197-1
Also available as an eBook.

Printed in the United States of America.

To the memory of my grandmother
Grace E. Young

CONTENTS

List of Maps

INTRODUCTION

THIS IS A BOOK ABOUT A BOOK. THE PARTICULAR TEXT WE ARE examining has been, regrettably, lost to the ages. No one has yet found even a shred of a copy of this work. Still, without even that we can attempt to piece it together. We can take short snippets from later books and formulate a sketch. We can get a feel for the author and tone and flesh it out. In the end, our picture will still be imperfect, but we'll have a nearly complete impression of a book that hasn't been read since ancient times, a firsthand account of Alexander the Great's campaigns, a book that we will call Ptolemy's *History of Alexander's Conquests*, or, to shorten it, Ptolemy's *History*.

Entire books have been written on the ancient texts that historians use when writing about Alexander the Great. The main texts are known by their authors: Plutarch, Curtius Rufus, Diodorus of Sicily, Justin, and Arrian. All of these were Roman-era authors who relied on earlier works. The earlier works, which are also known by their authors, are all lost: Nearchus, Aristobulus, Callisthenes, Cleitarchus, and Ptolemy. Of course, those are just the known texts, texts that have been mentioned by later writers. There remains the very reasonable possibility that there were other ancient texts about Alexander, texts that could be said to be contemporaneous or, at least, written in the hundred years after Alexander's death. All are lost except the Roman-era writing; not a scrap remains, or so it would seem.

The truth, and the reason for this book, is that with a little bit of literary forensics, one of those lost books can be recreated by using the Roman-era writings and by examining what we know about the author and the period in which the lost book was written. We don't know the exact name of the work, but we'll call it Ptolemy's *History* because that is who wrote it and that is, in essence, what it is: a history of Alexander's conquests, his battles, his triumphs and tragedies. It was written by someone who was at Alexander's side through it all, Ptolemy Lagides, or son of Lagus, who was eventually one of his seven elite bodyguards/advisers and a commander in the Macedonian army.

My approach to this task is simple. First, there are certain things that are known to have come from Ptolemy's book. The most common example is to be found in Arrian, when he writes, "Ptolemy, son of Lagus, says ..." There is a chance that Arrian misidentifies his source, or that a translator got it wrong. There is that chance, but it is a small chance, and it seems more likely that Arrian was fastidious in his citations and that translators were sure to get a proper name right rather than a common word. Thus, the words or figures that Arrian says come from Ptolemy would have indeed come directly from Ptolemy's *History*. It is a risk we must be willing to take. History is nothing but murky waters, in truth, and the farther back one goes, the murkier it seems to be. To go even farther, we must take what we know to have come from Ptolemy—that his focus was on military exploits, that he showed Alexander as a logical empire builder, and that he provided detailed accounts of the positioning and deployment of troops and figures on the losses during battle—and draw conclusions from it. Also, we can take what we know about Ptolemy and draw certain reasonable conclusions about him: that he became king of Egypt through Alexander's conquest and so was, perhaps, attempting to cement his power through the writing of his *History*, and that he had basically no reason to show Alexander in a negative light, unless he felt some obligation to remain truthful or accurate.

From these things we can determine what sorts of details are likely to have come from Ptolemy. It is speculation, but educated speculation. If I believe something is likely to have come from Ptolemy's *History*, I will say that it is likely and give the reasons why.

Ultimately, this book is about recreating something that has been lost as close as possible to what it may have been. I will not be recreating it verbatim, but instead providing a sketch of what the book was and how it showed Alexander; removing the

A bust of Alexander the Great, 2nd–1st century B.C., at the British Museum. (©*Andrew Dunn*)

Roman veil and getting at something a little closer to the truth. We'll never know what Alexander was really like, or for that matter Ptolemy. We can't know their inner thoughts, their unspoken doubts, or even the words they spoke. When we see a passage that is purported to have been spoken by Alexander, we must always ask ourselves: Did he truly say this, or is this the imaginings of later writers? If some Roman-era authors claim that Alexander thought something or was drawn to something, we must ask: How do they know? Often the answer is likely that they did not know. It is obvious but needs to be stated: there were no video cameras trained on Alexander during his great battles, no sound-recording devices turned on when he addressed his troops. Even if there had been, we would still have doubts. Did an editor take out all the negative incidents? Can any recording device truly capture the emotion of a moment? What of Alexander's inner thoughts? We have yet to find a secret diary written by Alexander himself.

One note on the main source for recreating Ptolemy's *History*, Arrian's *Anabasis*, which was written in the second century AD and covers all of Alexander's campaigns and conquests from the moment he became king of Macedon to his death in Babylon. Arrian led an interesting life himself, becoming Roman consul under Emperor Hadrian in 129 or 130 AD. He was governor over Cappadocia, which lies in Anatolia (modern-day Turkey), an area Alexander and Ptolemy would have been very familiar with. Arrian was a consummate author with many works to his credit. He not-so-modestly expressed the hope that he would be considered foremost in Greek letters, as Alexander was foremost in war. Setting his aspirations aside, as far as ancient sources go, Arrian is usually ranked as one of the better sources, and possibly the best, on Alexander because of his attempt at verisimilitude and because he not only chose good eyewitness sources, like Ptolemy, but he explained his reasons for choosing such sources. However, Arrian is not universally admired. One of his greater flaws was that he believed Ptolemy's *History* to be purely factual and doesn't acknowledge Ptolemy's obvious agenda.

Finally, even if I do not directly mention it, everything I describe that takes place during Alexander's conquest is something I believe comes from Ptolemy's *History*, unless I explicitly state otherwise. If I ignore some part of Alexander's history, most notably his childhood, it is because I do not believe that information was included in Ptolemy's work.

Now, let us retire to the Library of Alexandria.

one

THE LIBRARY OF ALEXANDRIA

THE LIBRARY OF ALEXANDRIA EXISTS IN NOTHING BUT LEGEND today, but at one time it was a real physical place. Built some twenty-three hundred years ago, it would have been, or would have been part of, a massive complex for its time. Believed to have housed hundreds of thousands of texts, it must have seemed a marvel. There is much that isn't known about the library, chiefly who built it, what it was really like, and exactly how many scrolls it held. The list of possible builders is short. It was either built by Ptolemy I, son of Lagus, of Egypt, or by his son, Ptolemy II. This places the construction of the library in about the third century BC.

Imagine if you will that you are a visitor to the library. Your sandaled feet pad over the newly carved stone steps. The day is bright and hot, and the sounds of the city are all around you. You enter through an open doorway and are thankful for the shade. Light comes in through openings in the roof, and you see the walls are honeycombed with slots for papyrus scrolls. You walk to a certain section, perhaps devoted to histories. You see Herodotus's and Thucydides's works. There is Callisthenes's history of Alexander the Great. And put in a place of importance is the work you are looking for, Ptolemy's *History of Alexander's Conquests.*

Of course, we don't know for certain that it was called *History of Alexander's Conquests,* or *History of Alexander,* or anything else for that matter. Sometimes it is called the *Ptolemaic Diary,* which is not to be confused with the *Royal Diary* of Alexander that is sometimes referred to by ancient writers. The problem, of course, is that the book has since been lost. No copy of it survives, and it is only mentioned, for the most part, in passing by later writers. However, we can glean the rough outline of our lost book. We know exactly who wrote it, for one thing: Ptolemy I. He is sometimes given the additional title of Ptolemy I Soter; *soter* is a Greek epithet meaning savior. He is also called Ptolemy son of Lagus or just Ptolemy Lagides, though who Lagus was remains something of a mystery.

Ptolemy was born in Macedon and grew up in the court of Philip II. He was a childhood friend of Alexander's and went with the young king on his conquests. He became one of his closest companions and most trusted generals. After Alexander died, he gained control of the wealthy territory of Egypt, where he eventually crowned himself king, or pharaoh. It seems that around this time he wrote a history of Alexander's campaigns, what we are calling Ptolemy's *History.* Sometime later, the Library of Alexandria was built, and it seems all but certain that a copy of the king's historical text was part of the collection.

It is not certain how many copies of the book were originally made. One would assume that other copies of the book would have been made over the centuries (it is impossible to say how many), but one by one they were all lost, destroyed, or otherwise erased. What we have left are tantalizing glimpses into one of the most compelling ancient stories ever recorded, that of Alexander the Great. Yet there is more to it than just that, because this lost book also seems to tell us something of its author, Ptolemy, and something of the Hellenization that followed Alexander's conquests. That spread of Greek culture and influence is seen not just in the pages of the lost book we are trying to reconstruct but also in the most likely home of this lost book, the Library of Alexandria, and in the very city where the library was built.

What Alexander found at the site is unknown. There was, by some estimates, little more than a fishing village there, with a small island lying off the sandy shore. Yet when he was traveling along the shore by the western branch of the Nile River in northern Egypt, he decided that this was the place for him to establish a great city. And great the city would be. He called it Alexandria, not one to shy away from self-aggrandizement. There is good reason to think Alexander was wise to choose the place he did because it was on the coast with room to build a harbor with access to the sea, and it was backed by a lake where a freshwater harbor could be constructed that would allow access to the Nile. Situated as the city was, it is not surprising that it did well. Moreover, Alexander picked a site that had no special importance to any group, allowing his new city to stand on its own, as it were, to be a Hellenistic city that could spring forth from the ancient land of Egypt. He also may have seen it as a city to rival and take the place of Tyre (in modern-day Lebanon), the greatest harbor in that region of the Mediterranean.

This last point is open to some discussion, however, because some have argued that after his establishment of Alexandria, Alexander may have felt he went too far by trying to replace Tyre and that Tyre was a more logical spot for a harbor. This coincides with a presumed shift in Alexander's thinking from being first and foremost the king of Macedon and the leader of the Greeks to being the heir to the Persian king and all the eastern lands in his domain. There is an argument to be made that had he lived, Alexander might have restored Tyre after it was sieged, and Alexandria would never have gained its prominence. But this is just the sort of speculation that one encounters when discussing Alexander and his intentions. What is known is that he founded Alexandria in a good location and left it to flourish.

Several years after Ptolemy gained control in Egypt following Alexander's death, Alexandria replaced Memphis as the capital of Egypt. It is hard to guess at Ptolemy's motive for making the change, but it almost certainly was viewed by most people as a clear shift in authority. The old capital was gone, the new authority was to be found in Alexandria, and it was a Greek or Macedonian authority. There Ptolemy established his court and his dynasty, and from there they would rule until the Romans came in the first century BC.

The city was designed by Dinocrates on a regular plan, with straight streets intersecting at right angles. It was built on a narrow neck between the Mareotic Lake and the marine harbor. In its Hellenistic heyday, it would have vibrated with the kind of energy that can only be found in a newly formed metropolis whose harbor and street life were the rivals of any other place on earth. A causeway was built to connect the island of Pharos, which lay in the harbor, with the shore. This causeway, in fact, created two harbors, one to the west, the other to the east. A very wide road ran down the center of the city from east to west and ended at two sets of gates that were later called the Gate of the Sun and the Gate of the Moon.

On Pharos was built the famous lighthouse that may have been as tall as 400 feet and was visible from thirty miles out to sea. This was completed by Ptolemy II, who had the honorific Philadelphus, meaning brotherly. On the eastern side of the east harbor sat the royal palace. As the Ptolemaic dynasty progressed, this area grew and expanded, eventually becoming a large complex. It is from here that Ptolemy I eventually ruled, and it is here that he might have written his *History*, hearing the waves and feeling the steady breeze of the sea.

The ancient writer Strabo, in his *Geography*, which was written some three hundred years after Ptolemy I reigned in Egypt, stated that a museum was part of the royal palace compound and housed a group of men of learning who "not only hold property in common but also have a priest in charge of the Museum, who formerly was appointed by the kings [of the Ptolemaic dynasty], but is now appointed by Caesar," referring to the Roman emperor. This museum, like the library, would have been a great center for learning, albeit under the control of the ruling monarch. In fact, the library might have been a part of the larger museum, which some historians believe contained gardens, a zoo, lecture areas, and shrines to the nine Muses, indicating that this was less a public library and more an exclusive archive that only a select few had access to. It has been estimated that at one point one hundred scholars lived and worked at the museum.

The library is believed to have housed something like five hundred thousand documents, most of them probably papyrus scrolls. The exact nature of the structure or structures that housed the museum and library are unknown. Probably the best-known part of the history of the library is that it was destroyed by fire. Yet this remains a mystery as well. One story claims that Julius Caesar destroyed the library when he set fire to ships in the eastern harbor. This was a tactical move in his pursuit of Pompey during the series of civil wars that would end the Roman Republic. By setting the ships on fire, he apparently inadvertently set part of the city on fire, and some historians believe this is when the library was destroyed. But there is no conclusive evidence to support this theory; no ancient sources actually point the finger at Caesar.

Another story says that sometime around the end of the fourth century AD, many of the library's documents were destroyed as part of a Christian conversion within the city. This is the story related in Edward Gibbon's famous *The Decline and Fall of the Roman Empire*. Yet still, there isn't a wealth of evidence to support this theory. Another possibility is that due to earthquakes, riots, conquest, conversion, and the inevitable march of time, the library simply didn't survive. Surely there would have been fires and reconstructions. Some of the contents of the library might have moved, changed hands, or been destroyed. Today a modern library exists in Alexandria and considers itself part of an ancient tradition, and rightly so. In that way, one could say the Library of Alexandria was never truly destroyed.

Many famous figures came out of the museum, including Heron of Alexandria, who was active in the first century AD (thus putting in great doubt the idea that Caesar destroyed the museum or library). He is famous as a mathematician, having a formula named after him that can find the area of a triangle by measuring its sides. He is also well known as an engineer, having invented various clever devices using water, one of them being a very early steam engine that was never realized for its practical uses. He also invented the world's first vending machines, in which a coin could be inserted and a portion of holy water would be delivered. He is also considered to have invented the first wind-powered devices for land.

Another such figure was Euclid of Alexandria, the famous mathematician. Ptolemy I was said to have been his patron. Euclid is considered the father of geometry, and his work *Elements* was used as a textbook for learning math for centuries. There is a famous anecdote in which Ptolemy I asked if there were a shorter path to learning geometry than Euclid's *Elements*. The mathematician replied, "There is no royal road to geometry." This story is questionable because similar stories have appeared between various kings and mathematicians, so it is hard to say where it originated.

Details about the museum, library, and the great thinkers of Alexandria give us an insight into Ptolemy and our lost book. Ptolemy I established a tradition that encouraged learning and research. Thus, these things could be considered important to him. So it would make sense for him to want to add his name to those authors reposited in his library. This does not mean Ptolemy was a king only concerned with the intellect. He was, in fact, a king of a conquered people.

Much like Rome, Alexandria had clear distinctions between citizens and noncitizens. First there were the Macedonians, who seemed to make up a special and elite class all to themselves. The rest of the citizens were Greeks and some Hellenized non-Greeks. They came from many areas, and while they all spoke Greek, they had a mix of dialects that must have made the early years of the city something of a struggle. Then there were Greeks who, for various reasons, didn't enjoy full citizenship. Next were noncitizens such as the Jews, who were numerous enough to have their own section of the city and created a community with their own organizations, officials, archives, and laws. There was also a large contingent of noncitizens from elsewhere in what is today called the Middle East, some of them holdovers from the Persian conquest of Egypt. Last, and this is a telling piece of information about what Egypt was like under Ptolemy's rule, came the Egyptians, those who had lived in the village before it became Alexandria and those who were ordered by Alexander to move to his new city from the Egyptian city of Canopus. They were also not considered citizens.

Under Ptolemy, Alexandria specifically and Egypt in general were bustling and productive. Egypt had always been a place of wealth and power. Under Ptolemy, Alexandria became its new center and would eventually become the greatest city and commercial center in the expanded Greek world. As any major city will do, it attracted thousands of people: poets, intellectuals, merchants, sailors, soldiers, farmers looking to sell their harvest, and tourists coming to see the latest marvels being constructed. Boats brought grains downriver from the productive Upper Nile Valley. They crossed large stretches of sea to bring in oil, figs, and honey from Greece, gold and ivory from Africa, spices from the Middle East, and products from faraway India. The city of Alexandria was a major producer of glass, linen, and papyrus.

One of the great marvels of Alexandria was Alexander the Great's tomb. After the young leader died in Babylon, his commanders, including Ptolemy, agreed on a burial spot for the

Macedonian king. It is not clear what spot they agreed on. Logically, they might have buried him in Macedon, near his father's tomb, but some historians think they wanted to bury him in the temple in the Oasis of Siwah in Egypt, where he was pronounced pharaoh and son of the god Ammon-Zeus. In any case, no ancient sources give Alexandria as the intended destination of Alexander's body, and it seems unlikely that it was, as this would have only have benefitted Ptolemy. The carrying of the body took two years to arrange and conduct in appropriate splendor and was entrusted to one Arrhidaeus. As Edwyn R. Bevan wrote in his interesting history *The House of Ptolemy:*

> Arrhidaeus, acting on an understanding with Ptolemy, set out from Babylon with the funeral cortege on the road to Egypt. If the body were taken to Siwah it would in any case (unless it went to Paraetonium by sea) have to go first to Memphis; it is likely that Arrhidaeus, on leaving Babylon, gave out the Oasis as his destination. Ptolemy met the cortege in Syria with a powerful escort, and took control. When it reached Memphis, it proceeded no farther towards the Oasis.

According to the Greek writer Diodorus Siculus, Ptolemy then brought the body to Alexandria. Pausanias, writing a hundred or so years after Diodorus, claimed that Ptolemy took the body to Memphis and it was his son who eventually brought it to Alexandria. However, most sources agree that it was Ptolemy I who brought Alexander's body to the city of his name, but it is unclear how long the body remained in Memphis before finally being settled in Alexandria.

Strabo indicates that the tomb was located in the Sema, which was an enclosed area attached to the royal palace where the kings of Greek Egypt were laid to rest near Alexander. This is fitting because it is through Alexander that they all derived their power, including and most importantly Ptolemy I. By placing Alexander's body next to his palace in his new capital, Ptolemy was sending a calculated message. What Alexander had created in Egypt, Ptolemy was maintaining. He placed the body in a gold coffin and enclosed it in a grand tomb, enshrining his power and status. As Peter Green puts it in his excellent *The Hellenistic Age: A Short History,* "burying one's predecessor was a royal duty and prerogative," meaning Ptolemy had visions of kingship.

Led by Perdiccas, the Successors (or Diadochi, as the various generals and important figures would be called) had agreed that Alexander should be taken by Arrhidaeus to a predetermined burial site that was most likely not the new city of Alexandria. By taking Alexander's body from Arrhidaeus, Ptolemy was openly disobeying Perdiccas, who played an important role in Alexander's conquests and was a key figure in Ptolemy's *History.* Perdiccas was the regent, ruling in place of Alexander's heirs: his mentally ill half-brother and his newly born son. Perdiccas had placed himself as head among the generals after Alexander's death, and it is believed that he must have struck a deal with Ptolemy, namely that Ptolemy would acknowledge Perdiccas as the regent if Ptolemy was given the prize of Egypt to govern. But it is clear that Ptolemy had no designs to remain under Perdiccas's rule and envisioned himself becoming a king in his own right. He was not alone in this regard. Almost all the generals given governorships after Alexander's death revolted against Perdiccas's rule and eventually declared themselves kings of their respective lands while trying to add to their kingdoms.

This period, often called the Hellenistic era, is a complex and confusing time and the subject of countless wonderful books. Our concern is with a book that was written at the very beginning of this era, and so it is good to get the lay of the land when Ptolemy's *History* was first published.

According to Diodorus, after Alexander's death, there was much confusion and threatening of war between the soldiers, the Successors, and the conquered, but eventually it was decided that Alexander's brother Philip Arrhidaeus (not to be confused with the Arrhidaeus who led Alexander's funeral cortege) would be king, Perdiccas would be his regent, and the "most important of the Friends and of the Bodyguard would take over the satrapies and obey the king and Perdiccas."

Perdiccas then split up the empire. The list of areas and the corresponding satraps is long and complicated, and it is not necessary to review it since it didn't last very long and these divisions were practically old history by the time Ptolemy wrote our lost book. Suffice it to say that Macedon was to be governed by Antipater; Anatolia (modern-day Turkey) was split into numerous areas with a wide array of governors, including Antigonus One-Eyed and Menander; Thrace was to be governed by Lysimachus; Seleucus was given the command of the cavalry of the Companions (a powerful position); and Ptolemy was to govern Egypt. Ptolemy was forty-four at this time.

By the time Ptolemy's *History* was written, Seleucus I (who was called Nicator, or the Victor) controlled a kingdom that covered part of modern-day Turkey, the eastern portion of the Persian Empire, and huge tracts of land reaching into Pakistan and India; Lysimachus held a kingdom in the western portion of Anatolia and Thrace; Cassander, son of Antipater, controlled Macedon and Greece; and Ptolemy still held Egypt and had added parts of the Levant and Asia Minor to his kingdom. Between those two periods—323 BC to 305 BC—there were endless wars and power struggles throughout Alexander's domain and beyond. The Greeks, led by Athens, revolted in the Lamian War and were quelled. Each of the Successors tried to outmaneuver the others. Perdiccas tried to gain control over everything and ended up dying in his quest to conquer Egypt, being killed by his own soldiers. Alliances were formed against any Successor who seemed to be grasping for too much, then these alliances would break up and infighting followed. Ptolemy was by no means an independent third party outside this quagmire; he was a constant and active participant. So when he decided to write a history of Alexander's campaigns, he was doing so as a scholar, but also as a Successor.

Unfortunately, there is no well-cited bibliography that we can read to get the particulars of our lost book, so determining the date that Ptolemy wrote his *History* is not easy, but we can narrow it down. Most of what can be known about the lost book can be gleaned from Arrian's *Anabasis*. In it, Ptolemy corrects a history of Alexander by Cleitarchus, which can be dated to 310–301 BC. Ptolemy died in 282 BC, so we know it must have come before then. There is strong reason to believe that Ptolemy wrote his autobiographical work at the turn of the fourth into the third century BC, let's say 305–295 BC. Ptolemy would have been in his sixth decade, an old man by the standards of the day, ready to write of his glorious and bloody years at Alexander's side.

The dating of Ptolemy's *History* is important because it places the work in the proper context of Ptolemy's looking to reaffirm his position as king of Egypt and head of a dynasty. His motivations then are clear. He hoped to correct any misgivings people may have had about Alexander or himself. He sought to establish his importance in the Alexander story while at the same time affirming Alexander's right of conquest. He was trying to promote his power as a progression from Alexander's power. Just as he sought to keep Alexander's body in his capital, he tried to enshrine Alexander's story the way he wanted it to be seen.

So we can assume he is not going to paint Alexander as a bloodthirsty megalomaniac or a man corrupted by his own power. However, Ptolemy does appear to avoid romanticizing Alexander or painting him as a tool of the gods. As historian Jona Lendering puts it in his article "Ptolemy I Soter," "in Ptolemy's view, Alexander had been a rational expansionist."

The question remains: Why recreate this lost book at all?

The answers to this are many and varied. One simple answer is that it can be done. So many works of antiquity have been lost to the ages that the chance to bring back even part of one is something that should be done. We are lucky in that Arrian tells us, directly at times, that he is using Ptolemy's *History* and that it is one of two of the main sources of his work. Since Arrian's *Anabasis* survives, part of our lost book survives.

Another answer to the question of why is because Alexander still intrigues us. Part of what makes him so appealing is the mystery that surrounds him. Many books and movies have tried to find the "real" Alexander the Great. This is exactly what Ptolemy was trying to do, show the world the "real" Alexander, or at least the Alexander that Ptolemy wanted the world to know. It would be a disservice to us to ignore a source like Ptolemy. While he is undoubtedly biased, his biases are easily known, because he was a well-known figure in his own right. There are truly no sources, especially ancient ones, who are completely free of bias, so it is good to get as many views on an ancient figure or time period as possible and try our best to extrapolate what truth we can.

One of the most obvious realities of researching Alexander is that all our ancient sources are from Roman times, when the republic and empire had taken control of the Mediterranean. Ptolemy represents something truly unique, a Greek point of view from the Hellenistic era. Not only that, but he witnessed many of the events he describes. He fought in the battles that he wrote about; he stood by Alexander's side as the king campaigned to the far reaches of the known world. Of course, Arrian's assurance that "Ptolemy not only campaigned with Alexander but, as a king himself, would have been particularly honor-bound to avoid untruth" seems a bit naive. As we progress through the book, I will let you test the veracity of that statement. Yet, having a leader, any leader, write of his times is something a historian would, or should, cherish. Moreover, Ptolemy's writing was important to ancient historians, at least to Arrian. And while Arrian may not be the finest historian or writer, he is probably one of the best sources and one of the most detailed we have on Alexander and definitely our greatest source for Ptolemy's *History*.

two

THE BEGINNING
OF PTOLEMY'S HISTORY

P TOLEMY'S HISTORY MOST LIKELY DIDN'T BEGIN WITH Ptolemy's birth, or Alexander's birth eleven years later. It probably didn't discuss Ptolemy and Alexander growing up in the Macedonian court, their youthful adventures, or any important life lessons. There was probably no mention of the time before Alexander's birth, of his mother Olympias and the later tales of her possibly being impregnated by a god. There would have been no mention of Alexander's actions as a teenager or his education by the great philosopher Aristotle. In all probability, it didn't include Ptolemy's exile from Macedon by King Philip II, Alexander's father (and possibly, as some speculate, also Ptolemy's father). The exile would have been a blemish on Ptolemy's record, and since he was writing a history of Alexander's conquests, it seems perfectly reasonable that he would want to exclude this from his narration and begin at a more convenient time. But it is worth mentioning and investigating his banishment, if only to add some shade to the character of our author.

Plutarch, the Roman biographer of the first century AD, relates from an unknown source that Ptolemy's exile stemmed from a proposed marriage. Pexodorus, king of Caria (in what is now southwest Turkey), offered his daughter in marriage to Philip II's other son, Philip Arrhidaeus. Arrhidaeus was Alexander's half-brother and is often described as mentally ill or somehow deficient; after Alexander's death, he would be used as a pawn by the Successors. Once again according to Plutarch, Alexander's friends, including Ptolemy, and his mother, Olympias, convinced the young prince that this marriage would elevate Arrhidaeus and be Alexander's undoing. Alexander must have taken the bait and sent an emissary to Pexodorus to convince the king that it would be better to form a marriage alliance with Alexander than Arrhidaeus. Pexodorus immediately saw the benefit in this. Philip II did not.

The king, his father, came to Alexander enraged and declared that he was unworthy to be Philip's heir if he would marry himself to a Carian—as Plutarch puts it, "a slave and subject to a barbarous king" (referring to the king of Persia, Artaxerxes IV, who ruled over Pexodorus). For his supposed role in convincing Alexander to undertake this calamity, Ptolemy and several others of Alexander's friends were sent into exile. Where they went is not entirely known. There's no clear mention in the historical record of when this all took place and how long Ptolemy remained in exile, but Alexander was surely not a young child when he boldly attempted to undermine his father's wishes. So let us say that for a few years, Ptolemy remained in exile. If so, his *History of Alexander's Conquests* most likely began after the death of a king.

If what Ptolemy wrote was a memoir or based mainly on his own memory, then to some extent we can assume he didn't discuss Philip II's assassination, as he wasn't present, being in exile at the time. Moreover, Ptolemy's *History* seems to be focused exclusively on Alexander's conquests, so all one needs to know is that Philip's death led to Alexander's becoming king of

Macedon. There is, of course, plenty of speculation concerning Philip's death. Someone, possibly the historian Cleitarchus, related that Philip was assassinated by a noble named Pausanias. It isn't clear if Cleitarchus or another later writer, perhaps Plutarch, first incriminated Olympias in her husband's death and then cast a suspicious shadow on Alexander himself, but this seems to be mere speculation and would certainly not show up in Ptolemy's *History.* It was not in Ptolemy's best interest to portray Alexander as the sinister hand behind his father's own death. As we will see, Ptolemy's main goal in his *History* was to show Alexander as honorable or, at the very least, a glorious leader, not a shadowy figure who had to pay an assassin to ensure his place on the throne.

So the lost book would probably have started in Macedon with Ptolemy being returned to Alexander's side, having been recalled from exile by Alexander himself. Then, almost immediately after Ptolemy's return from exile and Alexander's ascension to the throne, they would have been on the road, riding on a trail to Peloponnesus. They might have caught up with each other and reestablished their friendship. But there would have been little time for reminiscing. At twenty years old, Alexander was now king of Macedon and had to reaffirm the control that his father had obtained over the Greek city-states to the south. At this point, Ptolemy was not part of the seven elite bodyguards, but he would have been among the inner circle of the young king. It is safe to assume that throughout Alexander's campaigns, Ptolemy was either very near the king or off conducting the king's business. They traveled to Peloponnesus, or the Peloponnesian Peninsula, to meet with the League of Corinth and demand that the Greeks provide the same allegiance to Alexander as they had to his father.

For the most part, they would be successful. All the various city-states that made up the League of Corinth agreed to confer the power granted to Philip onto Alexander, except for the Spartans. It is reported by Arrian, who probably read it in

Aristobulus's or Ptolemy's accounts, that the Spartans refused because "it was not in their tradition to follow others but to take the lead themselves." The Athenians, on the other hand, might have considered opposing Alexander but were thrown off by his rapid march south from Macedon into Greece, and so they gave him even more honors than they had given Philip. Thus Alexander believed he had the capitulation of the Greeks, except for Sparta.

The Macedonians, Ptolemy among them, must have been concerned that with the death of Philip their domination and status might have crumbled. Perhaps Ptolemy didn't doubt his friend, but with this decisive action in Greece, Alexander proved that he could command the respect, at least at face value, of his various subjects. Of course, this would not prove the end of troubles in mainland Greece. For the time being, however, Alexander marched his army back up to Macedon for the winter, a prospect most of the soldiers likely didn't relish, for the winters of the Macedonian north are harsher than the mild climate of southern Greece.

Alexander then waited until the spring of 335 BC to launch a campaign into Illyria and Thrace, which bordered Macedon to the north and east respectively. First he met resistance from Thracians in a narrow mountain pass in the Mons Haemus (the modern-day Balkan Mountains in Bulgaria and Serbia). It is probably from our lost book that Arrian derives his description for this battle of the mountain pass.

The Thracians had aligned themselves at the top of the pass and used several wagons as a kind of blockade to stand behind. They also, apparently, had the idea of pushing the wagons down the mountain pass in the hopes of killing and putting into disarray their attackers. Alexander saw no other way but to break through this line in order to get over the mountain. He ordered that when the wagons came down the pass, those who could should stand out of the way and let them roll by. Those who couldn't do so should lie on the ground with their shields over them and let the wagons roll on top of them. This unique strategy worked perfectly: once the wagons began to make their way down the pass, the infantrymen did as they were ordered, and none died.

The army then took up a war cry at this immediate success, and Alexander rallied his troops and commanded them to attack. He placed archers to the right of his formation while he commanded from the left. In short order, they were up the pass and pushed back the Thracians from their position. The enemy then threw down their arms and ran off into the forest. Luckily for them they knew the land, and many were able to escape. But Alexander did take all the women and children as captives from this skirmish, along with all the valuables they had brought with them. In this first action as king, Alexander wasted no time, and he sent the booty and captives off to be sold.

Alexander then marched on the Triballi, a Thracian tribe whose land was primarily in modern-day Serbia, and reached the river Lyginus, where he met an army of Triballians as they were making their camp. The Triballians drew themselves up close to a wood that bordered the river. Alexander commanded his archers and slingers to start shooting at the enemy as a means of provoking them out of the wood and into open ground. The Triballians, seeing that the archers and slingers were unarmed aside from their bows and slings, charged at them and thus left the protection of the wood. Alexander ordered Philotas, son of Parmenion, to take a portion of the cavalry and charge the Triballians' right wing while another part of the cavalry hit the left wing. Alexander led the infantry phalanx, with the rest of the cavalry arranged in the center. This routed the enemy, who fled into the woods and toward the river. Arrian says that three thousand of the Triballians were killed, but only a few were captured. Ptolemy's *History* records that in all only eleven of Alexander's cavalry died and only forty infantry.

While Arrian only attributes the last figure to Ptolemy, it is almost certain that the entire account is covered in both

Ptolemy's and Aristobulus's histories. There is no account of any questioning or confusion in the battle on Alexander's side. Alexander is an unrivaled leader, and this may have been true, but there is very little to make him seem human. He is the hero of the story and thus is never unsure. Is this Ptolemy's propaganda, or is this truly who Alexander was? From his actions it seems certain that Alexander was not prone to doubts. He sees a threat to his power and he acts decisively and quickly. In the face of battle, he is coolheaded and commanding, just the sort of leader one hopes for in the chaos of war, especially the brutal disorder of hand-to-hand combat in ancient times. There is no questioning the fact that Alexander could lead and command his army. This, in some ways, makes Ptolemy's job easy. If he is trying to establish the authority of his rule in Egypt through the conquests of Alexander, it is that much simpler that Alexander exemplified many of the traits most sought by the ancient Greeks. He is brave, confident, and a born leader, traits that are valued even today. It is the negative traits and actions that Ptolemy must downplay in his *History.*

Next Alexander marched to the Danube River. Many Triballians and other Thracian tribespeople had taken refuge on an island called Peuce in the middle of the river. Alexander's warships had arrived up the Danube, and he tried to use them to force a landing on the island, but it proved too difficult. At this point, Alexander noticed a growing number of Getae on the other side of the river. "Getae" is a Greek name given to several Thracian tribes who lived along the Danube. Alexander decided to cross the Danube and attack the Getae. Arrian attributes this decision to a kind of yearning on Alexander's part to see what was on the other side of the river. This would seem to contradict the picture of Alexander as a calculating commander, and so it is possible that this did not come from Ptolemy's *History* but from some other source that Arrian didn't bother to name, or simply from Arrian's own imaginings. Then again, it could be that Alexander saw a chance for glory and also to ensure that the Getae would not cross the river against him.

With the cover of night, Alexander used dugout canoes and any other boat he could commandeer and crossed some fifteen hundred cavalry and four thousand infantry to the other side of the Danube. These figures are most likely from Ptolemy, but it must be remembered that Ptolemy used sources of his own. Here it may be that these numbers come from Callisthenes's official account of Alexander's conquests, which Ptolemy used in writing his *History.* Since Callisthenes was paid to flatter, it is possible that his figures are off the mark. But we have no way of knowing if he might have inflated these numbers to make Alexander's crossing of the river that much more impressive or if he deflated the numbers so that the eventual battle would be more impressive.

Whatever their number might have been, the troops landed on a bank of the river with some grain that had grown very tall. Using this as a cover, they advanced until they were out on open ground. Here the cavalry advanced to the side of the infantry and charged. According to Arrian, the Getae didn't withstand the first assault of the cavalry. They were taken completely by surprise. This once again demonstrates Alexander's tenacity and brilliance as a commander, and also his seeming lust for victory in battle. The Roman writer Diodorus Siculus, possibly drawing from Theopompus of Chios's *History of Philip,* stated that Alexander's father was said to be "prouder of his grasp of strategy and his diplomatic successes than of his valor in actual battle." If this is true, then one must wonder if Alexander shared the same view.

The Getae retreated to their city, also called Getae, possibly in the hopes that Alexander would not follow—but they were wrong. Seeing that Alexander was heading for their city, they abandoned it and fled into the countryside. Alexander's army took the city and carried off any booty that was left behind. Then Alexander gave the order to raze the city to the ground. It is worth noting that the razing of this city is seen as a short footnote in Alexander's conquest, while the eventual destruction of Thebes is shown in a much different light. This is easily explained, of course: the Getae were barbarians, the Thebans were civilized Greeks. We are not told why Alexander chose to burn this particular city to the ground, nor do we know what sort of city this might have been. But it is clear from Ptolemy, through Arrian, that Alexander gave the order to destroy the city. He alone was in command of how to settle the affairs of Getae.

After the sacking of Getae, Alexander brought his army back across the Danube to their camp. Next, ambassadors came to him from Syrmus, king of the Triballians, as well as representatives from some other Thracian tribes and also some Celts. The following details seem most likely to have come from Ptolemy or Aristobulus, since Arrian doesn't mention any other sources, but as we've seen, there is some doubt as to whether Arrian is fastidious about always citing his sources. It is a good story to note, but whether it comes from our lost book is highly uncertain.

Alexander received the ambassadors warmly and accepted their pledges of friendship. He asked the Celts what thing in the entire world they most feared, expecting that they would say Alexander himself. However, the Celts said they most feared that the sky would fall on their heads. Alexander took this answer in stride and let the ambassadors go, thinking of them as new allies, but he added later that the Celts were braggarts.

Alexander then marched into the land of the Agrianians, who had been allies of Philip's and remained so with Alexander. He was then given word that some of the Illyrians living north of Macedon had revolted and that a particular group, the Autariatians, were planning to attack Alexander on his way to Illyria. Around this same time, the king of the Agrianians, Langarus, came to Alexander with a contingent of troops to show his friendship. On hearing of the threat of the Autariatians, Langarus told Alexander not to worry, that he would personally defeat them. According to Arrian, this he did, and Alexander rewarded him with the hand of his half-sister, Cyna, in marriage. Unfortunately for Langarus, he died before he could wed Philip's daughter.

It seems highly likely that the above account comes from our lost book. It doesn't contain the flattering that is often associated with Aristobulus and has the matter-of-fact tone that seems to distinguish Ptolemy's account. Although it doesn't show Alexander as a commander, it does show him as generous to his friends, and this, as will be seen, is a key element to the propaganda of Ptolemy's *History.* It is this establishment of generosity that leads to the "this is what Alexander would have wanted" mentality that affirms Ptolemy's place on the throne in Egypt. Cyna, Alexander's half-sister, was not as lucky as Ptolemy: after Alexander's death, she was executed by Perdiccas, the regent in Macedon at the time.

Alexander then arrived at the city of Pelium, where the chief of some of the Illyrians, Cleitus, was stationed. There was a brief skirmish, and then the Illyrians retreated behind the walls of the city. Alexander camped near the city with the intention of laying siege to it, but another Illyrian commander, Glaucias, arrived with a large force at the same time. Thus Alexander was between the proverbial rock and hard place. If he attacked the city, then Glaucias would surely attack him; if he attacked Glaucias, then Cleitus would surely come to his ally's aid. The entire account of this battle almost definitely comes from Aristobulus and Ptolemy; most likely their accounts agreed in most places.

Alexander, seeing the situation for what it was, decided that the best option was an orderly retreat. First, he gave his phalanx a rapid succession of orders to impress the enemy within the city of the order and discipline of his troops. They advanced toward the river Eordaicus, which would be their escape. The Illyrians in the city came out to attack but were soon beaten back into the city. Next, Alexander and his so-called Companions, an elite and close-knit cavalry unit that was often under the direct command of Alexander, took a ridge that Glaucias had occupied with a small contingent. Ptolemy was surely a member of the Companions. (Ptolemy was also the name of a bodyguard who died early in Alexander's campaigns, and there was a Ptolemy who led some of the cavalry. There had even been a Ptolemy who was regent of Macedon three generations before Alexander. Obviously, Ptolemy was a common name.)

Alexander ordered his phalanx to cross the Eordaicus. Glaucias, seeing this as an opportunity, attacked the retreating foot soldiers. This is when Alexander ordered his cavalry to descend from the ridge they had taken and attack Glaucias. With archers firing from the middle of the river and catapults launching projectiles at Glaucias's army, Alexander was able to execute an orderly retreat without the loss of a single life.

Alexander then marched for three days until he had word that Glaucias and Cleitus were encamped at Pelium without sentinels or ramparts to guard them. Thus it is assumed that the Illyrians had believed Alexander had retreated out of fear and would not come back and attack them. So Alexander used the same tactic he had so successfully used against the Getae. With the cover of night he crossed back over the river and quickly attacked the Illyrians. Once again, the enemy was caught completely by surprise, and it is probably from Ptolemy's account that we learn that some of the Illyrians died while still in their beds. The enemy retreated, and Alexander chased them for some distance. Cleitus, Arrian says, set fire to the city of Pelium and retreated with the rest of the Illyrians. Many were killed and many were taken prisoner. Thus the rebellious Illyrians were defeated.

At some point around this time, Alexander received word that Thebes was making motions toward open revolt from Macedonian rule. According to Arrian and to Aelian in his *Various Histories,* part of what convinced the Thebans to revolt was the rumor that Alexander had died in Illyria. This story, according to Arrian, was given credit "because he had been absent a long time, and because no news had arrived from him." This story must be viewed with skepticism. Any story from the Theban revolt would first come through Macedonian sources— Callisthenes, Aristobulus, or Ptolemy—and it seems obvious that many excuses are made on both the Theban and Macedonian sides concerning the revolt, eventual battle, and aftermath. The Thebans most likely expected help from some of the other city-states. But Sparta and Athens withheld their support when Alexander's army arrived quickly to put a stop to the revolt.

Alexander knew that the Theban revolt was nothing to be trifled with. He marched his army at a breakneck pace and arrived within two weeks from north of Macedon to the outskirts of Thebes. In a recurring theme, we see Alexander's army appear suddenly and surprise the enemy. Alexander then encamped and gave the city a chance to send out an embassy. No doubt from Ptolemy's *History* comes the argument that Alexander did everything he could to avoid going to war with Thebes, that he gave it every opportunity to rebuke the few who had led it astray and embrace Alexander's rule. But it seems quite clear, even from Ptolemy's account, that what the Thebans wanted was independence. Anyone of the time and up to today could see this, but it benefits Ptolemy to have us think that it was wrong of the Thebans to revolt.

One of the constant motifs of Ptolemy's *History* is that Alexander's rule, Macedonian rule for that matter, is beneficial. Alexander is destined to rule the world, and the Macedonians, in particular Ptolemy, are destined to succeed Alexander. Through Alexander comes Ptolemy's hold in Egypt. The Thebans, according to Ptolemy, were wrong for wanting to rebel. They were swayed by exiles who secretly came to the city and incited them to revolt with lies about Alexander's death. Alexander, being the beneficent ruler, gave them a chance to mend their ways. Instead of sending an embassy, Thebes sent out some soldiers who attacked Alexander's camp. Alexander responded with some troops of his own, and the attackers were repelled.

The next day, Alexander moved his whole army to face one of the gates to the city. According to Arrian, most likely paraphrasing Ptolemy, Alexander didn't attack at this point. Perhaps there was a good tactical reason to hold off the attack; perhaps Alexander was waiting on word of any allies who might be coming to assist Thebes. But Ptolemy tells us something different. Once again, it was Alexander's magnanimity that kept him from attacking. He was still giving Thebes a chance to surrender peacefully. It refused. Directly from Ptolemy, we get a description of how the fighting began in Thebes.

With Alexander's army facing one of Thebes's main gates and positioned near a river, and with the Thebans behind blockades erected before the city walls, Alexander held his army at bay. But Perdiccas, one of Alexander's cavalry generals at the time, took it upon himself without a signal from Alexander to attack the Thebans and break through the first blockade. Another general, Amyntas, saw Perdiccas's attack and followed him. Alexander then saw that two of his units had been deployed without his order, so he sent in the rest of his army to assist them.

Ptolemy did an interesting thing here, and it might not be too bold to say he possibly rewrote history, or at least converted the truth to better suit him. The attack on and destruction of Thebes must have been something of a stain on Alexander's reputation. Thebes was a great and, above all, civilized and relatively free city. The fact that Alexander would wipe such a city off the face of the earth was probably unsettling and didn't match the vision of Alexander as a great spreader of Greek civilization. So it would be nice if he hadn't really started the fight. Instead, Ptolemy placed the blame on Perdiccas. The same Perdiccas who would, if the story is true, be given Alexander's signet ring on the king's deathbed. The same Perdiccas who would become regent in Macedon and would eventually wage an unsuccessful war against Ptolemy and lose his life in the struggle. When Ptolemy wrote his *History*, Perdiccas was probably long dead, but it would still benefit Ptolemy to cast Perdiccas as not honorable, attacking Thebes and, possibly even worse, disregarding Alexander's authority. Thus Perdiccas is someone of questionable character, and Ptolemy was in the right to, many years later, thwart him.

Perdiccas and his men made it to the second blockade, where Perdiccas was struck with an arrow and pulled from the battle. He suffered a grievous wound that took a long time to heal. Alexander's army pushed the Thebans back; the Thebans regrouped and responded in kind. Alexander then brought in his reserves and drove the Thebans back in through the city gates, which they were unable to close. The fighting continued within the city, and the Thebans were able to hold their ground for a while, but eventually Alexander's army overran them. With this, the Thebans broke and tried to escape as best they could.

Then there commenced a massacre, as Alexander's army fell on soldiers, women, and children. They killed people hiding in temples and in their own homes. Arrian, possibly getting his information directly from Ptolemy, tells us, "then indeed the Thebans, no longer defending themselves, were slain, not so much by the Macedonians as by the Phocians, Plataeans, and other Boeotians." It was generally known that these other Boeotians had been treated unkindly by the Thebans and that they were treated as subjects and not allies. So the Macedonians were once again let off the hook for the possible crimes committed against Thebes.

Alexander, according to Ptolemy's account, handed over the settlement of Thebes to the allies who had just engaged in slaughter. They, not surprisingly, decided to raze the city to the ground, split up the surrounding land between them, and sold all the surviving population into slavery. Plutarch gives the total number of slaves at more than thirty thousand. Given that in every other account throughout the campaigns it was Alexander who made the decision on what to do with a given city after being taken, this story stands out as possibly apocryphal. We must consider that this continues to fit within the theme of distancing Alexander from what occurred in Thebes. In fact, unlike his previous escapades in the north and his eventual adventures in the east, it seems Alexander was barely in control of this situation, and when he did have a chance to make a decision, he passed it off to vengeful allies. Yet even if this story were true and Alexander did let the Boeotians decide the fate of Thebes, he still must have known and sanctioned the destruction of the city and the selling of its inhabitants into slavery. Plutarch gives what seems to be a more reasonable explanation of events, stating that Thebes was destroyed "because Alexander expected that the Greeks would be terrified by so great a disaster and cower down in quiet."

If this was Alexander's reasoning, it appears to have worked. Very soon after the destruction of Thebes, the Arcadians, who had been on the verge of open revolt, put to death the revolutionaries in their midst. The Eleans called back exiles who had been supporters of Alexander. The Aetolians sent embassies to him, begging for pardon for their attempt to revolt. The Athenians, who were in the middle of celebrating the Great Mysteries of Demeter, stopped their sacred rituals and sent embassies to Alexander to show their support for all he had done and welcome him back to Greece. Alexander accepted their embassy with good will but asked the Athenians to hand over nine men whom he felt had helped instigate the unrest in Greece and were partially to blame for the Theban revolt. The Athenians begged him to reconsider, and he relented, asking only that one of the men be sent into exile.

three

CROSSING THE HELLESPONT

Alexander's army next returned to Macedon. There was a brief period of rest and recuperation, with the Olympic Games being held and religious rites observed. A curious omen was purportedly observed at this time. According to Arrian, a statue of Orpheus in Pieria began to sweat. Orpheus was a legendary figure in Greek mythology known primarily for his gifts as a musician and poet. This omen was regarded as a sign that Alexander would accomplish so much that the poets and musicians would work endlessly to record his great deed. This story of a sweating statue is a curious detail in Arrian's account, and he does not attribute it to any given source. Since Arrian says in Book 6 of his *Anabasis* that Ptolemy is "the main source I choose to follow," one might be inclined to automatically attribute anything not otherwise identified as being from our lost book. However, this assumption rests on a trust in Arrian to always attribute his sources, and we have no reason to have such faith in Arrian. Arrian did better than many ancient historians in attributing his sources, but we cannot be sure he always cites things accordingly. So the story of the sweating statue could be from any source.

Feeling he could now safely leave Greece, Alexander made his way to the Hellespont. There are two places where one can cross from Europe into Asia. Today they are both part of Turkey. The Aegean Sea lies to the west and the Black Sea to the east, and in the middle is the small Sea of Marmara. To each side of this smaller sea are the best places for crossing into Anatolia. The eastern side is the Bosporus and is where Istanbul currently sits, which would have been Byzantium in Alexander's time. The western strait is the Hellespont, and it is where Alexander chose to cross into Asia. He entrusted the management of Greece and Macedon to a general named Antipater. We are given numbers of soldiers that Alexander crossed with, and these almost certainly come from our lost book. Alexander had thirty thousand infantry and five thousand cavalry.

Our lost book would tell us that Alexander was the first off the ships upon crossing into Asia, he was in full armor, and he erected altars to Zeus, Athena, and Heracles (Hercules to the Romans) to give thanks for the safe crossing and in hopes of some protection in his campaigns. He then went to Ilium, a Greek city on the western coast of Anatolia, and sacrificed to the Trojan Athena. He also set up a panoply, a display of arms, as a votive offering. In exchange he took a set of armor that had been preserved from the time of the Trojan War. He had his shield bearers carry these arms in front of him during battle. This is part of a pattern that our lost book presents to show Alexander in a certain light. He observes the correct religious customs or precedence but then turns it to his own advantage. He paid homage to the Trojan Athena but then came away with important relics that he could use as a powerful symbol. Also at Ilium, Alexander placed a garland around the tomb of Achilles, and his favorite companion, Hephaestion, placed one on the tomb of Patroclus, who was the beloved cousin of Achilles. Alexander marched forward from Ilium and bloodlessly captured the city of Priapus.

Here we enter into shaky ground for our lost book. If Arrian drew information about what the Persians were doing at this point from Ptolemy's *History*, then one must wonder where Ptolemy got his information. There would have been accounts from the Persian camp; perhaps Alexander had spies already in place, though nothing is said to indicate this. After the battles were over, stories would have been told by enemy soldiers who had been captured, and this might have been where Ptolemy picked up information he wrote down years later. Of course, he could have also gotten the data from other histories, just as Arrian could have done. In any case, we must remain highly skeptical of the following story.

Arrian tells us that the Persian army closest to Alexander was encamped near the city of Zeleia, which is mentioned in the Iliad as being allied with Troy. The Persian generals were Arsames, Rheomithres, Niphates, Spithridates, Memnon, and Arsites, a governor. They had received word that Alexander had crossed the Hellespont with a large force. Memnon, who is often portrayed as the greatest of the Persian generals, advised against risking battle, since the Macedonians had the larger infantry and had the benefit of having their king with them, while King Darius III, who had come to the Persian throne in 336 BC (the same year as Alexander), was not with the Persian force. Memnon's strategy was to destroy all the land and fodder in Alexander's path, thus depleting his hope for a steady source of food and supplies. The governor, Arsites, could not agree to this as he didn't want any of the homes of the people he governed to be destroyed. It is said that the other Persians agreed with the governor, and Memnon was overruled. Diodorus says Memnon wished to lead an army into Greece and Macedon. This idea must have also been rejected.

Alexander then marched to the river Granicus, ready for battle. His scouts found the Persians aligned on the other side of the river in battle formation. The question then fell to Alexander whether he should have his army cross the river to meet the

Persians or wait. Here Arrian gives a conversation in stilted language between Alexander and one of his top commanders, Parmenion, concerning how the Macedonian army should handle the situation. There is no clear indication that this is from our lost book, but it does fit with some of the hallmarks of Ptolemy's *History*. For one thing, it is reasonable to think that Ptolemy's account would have been something of a memoir, and so it would have been likely that he included snippets of conversation as he remembered them. The dialogue does have the feel of a conversation remembered from a long time ago and not a verbatim dictation. Also, it casts Parmenion in an unfavorable light, and this will be important later in Ptolemy's book. We've seen already that Ptolemy is quick to cast an adverse light on those he thinks unworthy of Alexander's company. Parmenion spoke first:

> I think, O king, that it is advisable for the present to pitch our camp on the bank of the river as we are. For I think that the enemy, being much inferior to us in infantry, will not dare to pass the night near us, and therefore they will permit the army to cross the ford with ease at daybreak. For we shall then pass over before they can put themselves in order of battle; whereas, I do not think that we can now attempt the operation without evident risk, because it is not possible to lead the army through the river with its front extended. For it is clear that many parts of the stream are deep and you see that these banks are very steep and in some places abrupt. Therefore the enemy's cavalry, being formed into a dense square, will attack us as we emerge from the water in broken ranks and in column, in the place where we are the weakest. At the present juncture the first repulse would be difficult to retrieve, as well as perilous for the issue of the whole war.

It is impossible to imagine this long, well-thought-out thesis pouring from Parmenion's mouth in real life. Rather, it sounds like someone's summary of arguments against attacking the Persians immediately. Alexander didn't consult just one person when deciding his strategy, so it seems these arguments were all attributed to Parmenion. Alexander's response also has the feel of a distillation of the reasons to attack:

> I recognize the force of these arguments, O Parmenion; but I feel it a disgrace, if, after crossing the Hellespont so easily, this paltry stream should bar our passage for a moment. I consider that this would be in accordance neither with the fame of the Macedonians nor with my own eagerness for encountering danger. Moreover, I think that the Persians will regain courage, in the belief that they are a match in war for Macedonians, since up to the present time they have suffered no defeat from me to warrant the fear they entertain.

If this exchange came from the *History*, and it seems plausible that it did, then we can determine a few things. First, Alexander had intelligence on the morale of his enemy. This would be a key asset, and, as we continue in the narrative, it can be gleaned that one of Alexander's strongest tools was his intelligence on his enemy and his use of that information. Second, it seems fairly certain that Ptolemy would have been part of this war council, and while we have no way to know which argument he favored at the time, it is fairly apparent which argument he later saw as in the right. He put the arguments for bravery, glory, and daring in the mouth of Alexander, even though we have no way of knowing what Alexander's initial thoughts were upon coming to Granicus.

Unsurprisingly, the Macedonians marched forward and crossed the river. Fitting his rank, and despite his supposed arguments against the advance, Parmenion was sent to command the left wing of the army, with Alexander commanding the right. Cavalry and infantry were spread about, with archers and javelin throwers in the right wing. Alexander called the charge, and the first Macedonians across the river were cut to pieces by the Persians. But Alexander's right wing was not deterred, and it continued to cross, giving the Persians fierce battle. Eventually the Macedonians were able to push the Persians back, and the reason given is almost certainly from our lost book. The Macedonians had the advantage of fighting with cornel-wood lances while the Persians had simple light javelins.

These lances, or *xyston*, were nothing to be scoffed at. Reportedly measuring about thirteen feet long, they had points at both ends and were often aimed directly into the face of the enemy's horse with the hopes of causing the beast to rear up. Since cavalry at this time had no saddles or stirrups, they would have been knocked off their mounts. Compared to a javelin, which was probably a little over three feet long, the Macedonian cavalry would have had four times the reach of its enemy. These differences seem staggering, but even if we assume the Macedonian lances were on the short side and the Persian javelins were on the long side, there would still be significant inequalities. This difference could have easily stuck with Ptolemy, as he was most likely a part of that cavalry charge. When he sat down to write about it decades later, it must have been one of the key differences he could recall between himself and the enemy.

During this cavalry fight, Alexander's own lance was broken. He was given a new one and charged at Mithridates, the son-in-law of Darius, and "threw him to the ground with a thrust in the face," as Arrian puts it. At this time, the Persian Rhoesaces hit Alexander in the head with his scimitar and sheared off part of the king's helmet. Alexander responded by throwing Rhoesaces to the ground and driving his lance into the Persian's chest. Another Persian, Spithridates, was approaching Alexander with raised scimitar when a cavalryman named Cleitus, son of Dropidas, also called Cleitus the Black, cut off Spithridates's arm while it still held the scimitar aloft. One wonders if Ptolemy witnessed this scene himself. It seems more than probable. Since he was part of the cavalry and closely linked with Alexander, he most likely would have been very close to the young king's side. Arrian's other main source was Aristobulus, and while it is possible that author wrote these sorts of battle details, it seems more in line with Ptolemy that he would show Alexander in real mortal danger.

While Alexander was thus engaged, wave after wave of the Macedonian army crossed the Granicus and eventually turned the Persian force. It gave way first where Alexander was and then steadily down the line, until it had been completely routed. A thousand of the Persian cavalry were killed; the rest were allowed to flee. Alexander turned his attention to the Greek mercenaries who had been part of the Persian army. He surrounded them and massacred many of them while taking two thousand prisoners. The first true battle with the Persians had been won, and Alexander could stand glorious in his victory. Besides the commander Alexander had killed, Mithridates, and the one Cleitus the Black had killed, Spithridates, about six other leaders were killed. Memnon was able to escape, as was Arsites, the governor who couldn't stand for his people's homes to be destroyed, but it is said he committed suicide shortly after the battle.

Ptolemy's *History* is probably here cited for stating that only eighty-five of the cavalry died and only about thirty infantry. This seems an unbelievably small number and is very likely an exaggeration on Ptolemy's part, as he wanted to make the victory seem that much more impressive. However, Arrian tells us specifically that twenty-five of the so-called Companion cavalry died and that twenty-five bronze statues were commissioned in their likeness to be set up in Dium, so that number could be easily proven by a visit to the site in ancient times. The Greek mercenaries who were captured were sent to hard labor in Macedon as punishment for taking up arms against their fellow countrymen. Alexander sent three hundred sets of Persian armor to Athens to be dedicated to Athena on the Acropolis with the inscription, "Alexander the son of Philip and the Greeks except the Spartans dedicated these spoils from the barbarians occupying Asia." The slight to Sparta was intentional, as they had rejected the peace with Alexander after Thebes.

Alexander next marched toward the city of Sardis (modern-day Sart), but was met by the commander of the citadel's garrison eight miles outside the city so that the commander could peacefully hand the city over to Alexander. Alexander camped two miles from the city and sent Amyntas, son of Andromenes, to take over the citadel. Alexander marched on to Ephesus, famed for its Temple of Artemis, one of the Seven Wonders of the Ancient World. Here he restored the exiles who had been banished from the city for supporting him, broke up the oligarchy that ruled the city and installed a democracy, and ordered that the taxes that had been paid to the Persians instead be contributed to the temple. It is impossible to say if this account comes from Ptolemy, but it fits with the image of Alexander as a restorer of order. It is important to note that while some writers might have made much of Alexander's installing a democracy, there is no reason to think Ptolemy would have had much reason to encourage this sort of behavior. He was, after all, a monarch just like Alexander, and while it might have benefitted Alexander to create a localized democracy in one city as a means of showing his Hellenistic attitudes, it was not in Ptolemy's interest to have any democracies show up in Egypt. Of course, this gets at another layer to Ptolemy's *History*, and that is that he would not have been writing his book for a general audience.

The average Egyptian could no more read a copy of his book than he could spontaneously grow a pair of wings. For one thing, Ptolemy's book would have been in Greek, and for another, it would have been for the literate and more scholarly audience of Greek intellectuals and nobles. As has been mentioned, it is impossible to know how many copies of our lost book were around at any given time. We can only say for certain that Arrian was able to get a copy of it. But in his citing of Ptolemy, he does not give the impression that it was a popular or widely held book. If, in fact, Ptolemy's book was not widely known, it may be that Arrian cited from it in an effort to keep Ptolemy's writing from being lost. Of course, this is conjecture. Ptolemy might have wanted to idealize Greek virtues such as democracy, all the while expanding his kingly powers.

Next Alexander's army set out for Miletus. The outer city had been abandoned, so Alexander camped there with the hopes of besieging the inner city. The commander of the garrison in Miletus had earlier sent a letter of surrender to Alexander but had changed his mind because the Persian fleet was close by and possibly able to offer support. However, a Macedonian officer named Nicanor (possibly Nicanor of Stageira) brought up the Greek fleet with one hundred sixty ships and blocked off the harbor for the Persian fleet, which numbered four hundred. At this point there was another supposed debate between Parmenion and Alexander, with Parmenion once again on the losing side. Parmenion, it is said, argued for a sea battle, stating that there were divine signs of a victory on water. He is supposed to have said that a victory by the fleet would be a great boost, while a defeat would not be a serious setback. Alexander saw the deep flaws in this plan, namely that the numbers and experience clearly favored the Persian fleet. Alexander would not expose his small navy without a guarantee of success, despite the fact that at Granicus he was prepared to risk it all with no such guarantee. As one would expect, Alexander's arguments won out.

These debates with Parmenion seem to represent something more complex and true to life—the fact that Alexander held frequent war councils where ideas for strategy were shared and debated. It seems natural that the final decision would fall on Alexander, but it seems highly unlikely that the councils were only between the king and Parmenion, with one always being right and the other always wrong. Instead it is more realistic to think of these as something akin to the dialogues of Socrates. Parmenion represents the side that will eventually lose, and Alexander represents the side that will be chosen. But it is impossible to say who actually took part in these councils and what the conversations were really like. It is likely that Ptolemy attended many of them.

Outside Miletus, a representative of the leading men of the city offered, as Arrian puts it, "equal access to their walls and harbors for both Alexander and the Persians, and request[ed] that on those terms the siege should be lifted." Alexander promptly told the man to return to the city and prepare for war. Siege engines were built and applied to the walls. A part of the wall was broken down, and Alexander readied his army to go over it and attack the city. The Persian fleet could only look on from a distance, as Alexander's fleet blocked off the city from help. The Macedonians entered the city and immediately routed the Milesians and mercenaries trying to protect it. Many of the soldiers jumped into the city's harbor or went out in boats and were quickly stopped by the Greek navy. Arrian states that Alexander released the Milesians who didn't die in the capture of the city and offered the mercenaries the option of joining his army. Diodorus, however, explains that all the rest, meaning non-Milesians and nonmercenaries, were sold into slavery. It would be expected that Ptolemy might focus on Alexander's treatment of the Milesians and avoid discussing the fate of the others, and this would explain Arrian's silence on the matter of slavery.

Alexander then harassed the Persian fleet from land, cutting it off from its supply of water and effectively besieging the ships. After leaving, returning, and failing to get the Greek navy to come out into open water, the Persian fleet left, accomplishing nothing. After this, Alexander disbanded his own fleet, save for a handful of ships to carry siege engines. Diodorus puts it succinctly: "There are those who say that Alexander's strategic concept was sound, when he dismissed his fleet. For Darius was still to be reckoned with and there was bound to be a great battle, and he judged that the Macedonians would fight more desperately if he deprived them of all hope of escape by flight." However, this is not the reason Ptolemy gave for Alexander's disbanding the fleet. His reasons were more practical: a lack of funds for upkeep of the ships and a realization that his fleet was no match for the Persian fleet, which was much larger and manned with experienced seamen. While Ptolemy's reasons are in line with a more positive view of Alexander, there is also some logic behind them. Indeed, Alexander's fleet was no match for the Persians, and if the Greeks desired to retreat, they did not need a massive fleet to accomplish it, but a few boats to ferry them back across the Hellespont. Regardless, it is clear that Alexander, probably after some consideration, decided he would defeat the Persians by land and only by land.

Next came the siege of Halicarnassus, home to another ancient wonder, the Tomb of Mausolus (from which we get the word "mausoleum"). Like Miletus, Halicarnassus (modern-day Bodrum in Turkey) was a coastal city, and it had strong defenses as well as a naturally strategic position. The Persian general Memnon was in the city and had recently been made commander of Lower Asia and head of the entire navy, which was now blocking the harbor and ready to provide help to the residents of Halicarnassus. Alexander prepared for a long siege.

The days went by with a few brief skirmishes and trading of arrows and the like, but nothing in the way of a full battle. Alexander moved around the city, looking for the best approach to assault it. He traveled to the neighboring city of Myndus with a contingent of troops in the hopes he could capture that city with ease, but he found it too difficult and returned to Halicarnassus. He filled in the moat of the city in order to better position his siege towers. The soldiers within the city tried to burn the towers but were beaten back and failed in the attempt.

Arrian, undoubtedly drawing from Ptolemy's *History*, relates the following detail. Two Macedonian hoplites, in the midst of drinking and boasting, decided to prove their prowess by donning armor and attacking the wall of the city themselves. It is noted that these men came from Perdiccas's brigade, and so reflect poorly on Perdiccas, that villain-in-waiting who would one day make war on Ptolemy. Despite being outnumbered and on lower ground, the two drunken hoplites began to kill any of

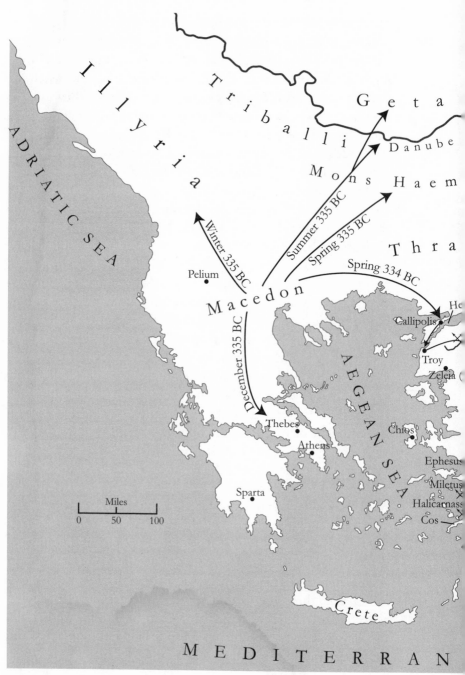

Map 1. Alexander's route through Ancient Greece and Anatolia.

River

us

c e

ellespont

Granicus River

(?)

BLACK SEA

N

Gordium

P h r y g i a

C a p p a d o c i a

Sagalassus

Pisidia

Cyndus River

Battle
of
Issus

Milyas

Termessus

P a m p h y l i a

Tarsus

Hyparna (?)

Aspendos

C i l i c i a

Myndus

Soli

Magarsus (?)

Telmissus

Pinara

L y c i a

Mallus

Xanthus

Patara

C y p r u s

E A N   S E A

the Persian soldiers who came to meet them. At this point, more
of Perdiccas's men came out to join in the fight, once again
showing that propensity to rash action. However, Arrian notes
that in this short battle, the city came close to being captured,
and it is left to speculation if this insinuation comes from
Ptolemy, Aristobulus, or somewhere else altogether. Regardless,
the city did not fall.

A section of the wall between two towers was knocked down,
but the Persians built a new wall in its place before Alexander's
army could advance through the opening. The Macedonians
brought in their siege engines against this new wall, and once
again there was an attempt to set these on fire. The fires were put
out, and Alexander came to rally his troops at this spot. Still they
were unable to break into the city. A few days later, Alexander
attacked this same location, obviously seeing it as the greatest
weakness. In the meantime, the Persians attacked at another gate
where few Macedonians were stationed and did not expect an
attack. This attack was met by Ptolemy the royal bodyguard—
once again, not to be confused with the author of the lost
book—who died in the struggle but was able to repel the
Persians and force them back into the city.

At this point we are told that Memnon and the other Persian
satrap of the region, Orontobates, decided they could no longer
hold the city. They ordered a portion of the city and some of
their temporary battlements burned. Both Arrian and Diodorus
agree that Alexander finished the job by razing the city once it
was completely in Macedonian hands. Thus Halicarnassus fell.
Alexander then left the city with a garrison and set out for
greater Phrygia, a kingdom to the north and east. It should be
noted here that Halicarnassus was the capital of the kingdom of
Caria, which was conquered by Persia but allowed to retain its
monarchy, though it appears to have been a puppet monarchy
controlled by the Persians. It should be remembered that the
governor/king of Caria before Orontobates, Pexodorus, had
been the one to offer a marriage alliance with Alexander's half-

brother, which had led to Ptolemy's exile. In order to subdue the rest of Caria, Alexander left a force of three thousand mercenary infantry and two hundred cavalry under the command of another Ptolemy, not our author.

There followed two actions by Alexander, the reports of which seem certainly to have come from Ptolemy's *History*. In the first, Alexander restored the Carian satrapy to one Ada, a woman who previously had control of Caria but had presumably had it stolen from her by Pexodorus, who was Orontobates's father-in-law. Ada went to Alexander when he marched into Caria, offered her friendship, and asked that she be allowed to call him her son. Alexander agreed to this and restored the satrapy to her as a reward for her friendship. The reason this seems to be taken from the *History* is that it continues the theme of Alexander as a force for righting wrongs, for settling the abuses committed by the Persians. This is, of course, something of a stretch. We cannot know, for instance, whether Ada was a good satrap/queen or a poor one, and it seems possible that Alexander had little idea himself. We do know that Alexander's decision would be overturned, like so much else, upon his death.

In his second reported action after the fall of Halicarnassus, Alexander sent some of the Macedonians home for the winter. The reason given in Arrian, and so plausibly the reason given by Ptolemy, was that many of his men were newly married and wanted to spend time with their new wives. He sent them back with yet another Ptolemy (also not our author) and two generals, Coenus, son of Polemocrates, and Meleager, son of Neoptolemus, who was also recently married. Alexander told them that when they returned, he hoped they would have recruited as many cavalry and infantry as they could from Macedon. We are told that letting some of his men go home to be with their new wives did much to ingratiate him to his men.

There is no discussion of these matters in Diodorus or Plutarch, and that is not surprising, as neither had the time in their shorter narratives for what might seem to be trifling matters. But neither of those writers used Ptolemy's *History* as a main source, so they might not have read of Ada or of the newly married Macedonians. The first thing that is clear about these stories is that there is no mention of any discussion on the matters, in the manner of the Parmenion dialogues, and so we are led to believe that Alexander acted without counsel. Seeing the wrongs done by the Persians, Alexander corrected them and installed Ada as satrap. No one needed to explain the history and local customs to Alexander, for instance, that it was accepted that women could become ruling monarchs, unlike in Macedon. Understanding that his men needed to see their wives, Alexander sent them home with gratitude for the season. No one needed to petition the king for his soldiers to have these months of leave. One wonders what the bachelors and long-married men of the Macedonians thought of their comrades as they packed up their things and marched away. In these two instances, Alexander seems the very model of a good king and commander, which is just what Ptolemy hoped to convey.

four

CONQUERING ANATOLIA

ONE DAY DURING THE SIEGE OF HALICARNASSUS, ALEXANDER lay down to rest on a couch that was provided for him. It was outside, in the open air, and laying in the warm sunlight he fell asleep. A swallow then flew down and perched itself on the couch and began to make such a racket that others near the king took notice of the bird and were surprised when Alexander didn't awaken at the noise. The bird flew around the king, alighting all over the couch and on Alexander. The king batted at the thing in his sleep, but the bird was not perturbed. It was not until the bird perched on Alexander's head and continued its loud chirping that the king finally woke up and the bird flew off. Later, Alexander asked a soothsayer if there were any omens to be taken from such a thing. The soothsayer, Aristander the Telmissian, replied that it meant one of Alexander's friends was plotting his death, but that the plot would be discovered.

After Halicarnassus, Alexander took his army to the regions of Pamphylia and Lycia on the southern coast of modern-day Turkey in order to capture all the cities there and, according to Arrian, "by that means render the enemy's fleet useless." The

Persian fleet would be unable to get supplies from these cities and so would be unable to stay in the waters near Turkey. Arrian makes a point to state that Alexander undertook this campaign during the winter, but this wouldn't have been much of a winter by Macedonian standards. In these early campaigns, it seems Ptolemy must have had little to say about the weather or even the condition of the men. The pace that Alexander demands is a formidable one, but we must remember that Ptolemy would have been on a horse and might not have known much about the toll of this constant warfare on an average foot soldier. Regardless, Ptolemy does not appear to do much in the way of complaining in his *History*. It is more about the glory of Alexander and the glory of Ptolemy than about the day-to-day trials of a soldier's life.

Alexander's army marched first to Hyparna, in Pamphylia; we are told that it was a well-fortified city, manned with a garrison of Greek mercenaries. It isn't quite clear where Hyparna was exactly or what modern-day city it may correlate to, if any. The distinction of this place is that Alexander was able to take it with ease and then allowed the Greeks to leave in peace. This is important to note because Alexander was not always so forgiving to Greek mercenaries who fought for Persia. It seems that at times when it suited him, he let these mercenaries go, while at other times they might have lost their lives.

Next Alexander went into the region of Lycia, which Strabo tells us is "rugged and hard to travel, but is exceedingly well supplied with harbors and inhabited by decent people." Decent people or no, it was a land that Alexander meant to conquer. He immediately took the largest city in Lycia, Telmessos. In quick succession he took Pinara, Xanthus, Patara, and a scattering of other small towns. The battles, if there were any, would have been small affairs; the towns would have had little defense in the face of Alexander's army and probably knew their fate before the Macedonians arrived. Many, if not all of them, capitulated before any blood was shed. Alexander then went to Milyas, a region that paid tribute to Lycia based on an agreement set up by the Persians. Here many envoys approached Alexander's army to offer him their friendship and crown him with gold. Alexander accepted these people and commanded them to surrender their cities to whoever he sent to govern them. Everyone, probably not surprisingly, agreed.

Unbeknownst to Alexander, a plot to assassinate him was, in fact, developing around this time. Ptolemy may be the source for this story, but most of what he heard about the plot would have been hearsay. The details we have are that one of Alexander's officers deserted and went to the Persian side, to Darius. He brought with him a letter from another officer, one Alexander, son of Aeropus. The letter, it is believed, said something that indicated this Alexander was willing and able to kill the king Alexander. Darius then dispatched a courtier to meet with the treasonous Alexander and tell him that if he were able to kill the young king, Darius would appoint the assassin king of Macedon. The plan failed, however, for the courtier was captured by Parmenion. When the plot was revealed, many reminded Alexander of the omen that Aristander had seen in the noisy swallow. Arrian tells us that Alexander called a council to discuss what should be done with the traitor. It is likely that this detail comes from our lost book, as Ptolemy would have been part of this council.

This part of the story is interesting because it shows Alexander deliberating with a group over a decision and not reaching the apparently immediate decisions he had previously made without counsel. It leads one to wonder if calling a council was not a more common occurrence than is described in Ptolemy's *History* and the other ancient texts. The Companions—again, we assume Ptolemy was one of them— were all in favor of "putting him out of the way." The sources are not clear if this meant putting the would-be assassin to death or simply relieving him of his command and arresting him. In the end, the son of Aeropus was arrested and put under guard. It seems highly likely that the story of the treasonous Alexander comes from our lost book. It was something that Ptolemy witnessed—at least the debate among the Companions as to the fate of the traitor—and Arrian would have likely used the tale knowing that it was, in part at least, an eyewitness account.

Alexander then marched along the coast and was met by a delegation of Aspendians, coming from the city of Aspendos. They offered to surrender their city to Alexander as long as he didn't install a garrison there. Alexander agreed, provided the Aspendians handed over a tribute of fifty talents and all the horses the city had been breeding for Darius. The Aspendians agreed and left to return to their city with the promise of bringing back the money and horses. Alexander then conquered the city of Side and installed a garrison there. He was ready to move on to the next city when word reached him that the Aspendians were refusing to meet their side of the agreement and were making preparations to defend their city against him.

At Aspendos, Alexander found a well-fortified inner city closed against him. He was not inclined to use the time and manpower that would be required to lay a siege, but seeing few options, he camped around the city. The Aspendians, on seeing Alexander's force, must have reconsidered their preparations for defense, for they sent out an envoy requesting that they be allowed to surrender the city under the previous terms. Alexander refused and presented new demands. He asked for one hundred talents instead of fifty, the horses previously promised, hostages of their most influential men to guarantee they would obey whatever viceroy he placed over them, and an annual tribute to the Macedonians. The Aspendians agreed.

One must wonder what the leaders in these various cities were thinking when dealing with Alexander. How many of them must have thought that any agreements they made with the young king would be overturned once Darius defeated this upstart? How many of them saw in Alexander their future? None of them could have guessed the fate of their city in ten or twenty years' time, the succession of kings and wars that would mark the age. They had to deal with immediate problems, such as a massive army stationed around their city walls, ready for battle. So they treated with the king and gave him whatever he wanted.

Our lost book then tells us that Alexander marched toward Pisidia, a region north of Lycia in southern Anatolia. This account truly could have come from Ptolemy, Aristobulus, or perhaps most likely both. Alexander's army came to the city of Termessus, which rested in a high place with precipitous drops on all sides of the city. Two large ridges rose on each side of the road into the city and so formed a natural gate, making it easily defendable. Alexander had his army positioned near this gate. The Termessians withdrew from beyond the city walls into the city and left a small guard on the gate. Alexander attacked the guards with missiles from his archers and javelin throwers. In short order, the guards abandoned their position, and Alexander was able to enter through the gate. He was then approached by the Selgians, a group of people from the region who were long-standing enemies of the Termessians. He made allies of these people.

According to Arrian, Alexander then decided he did not want to waste time trying to capture Termessus. Since this is a direct statement of Alexander's intent, it is probable that this came from Ptolemy and may reflect Alexander's true thoughts on this occasion. Instead, Alexander marched to another city, Sagalassus. Here he found defenders on a hill in front of the city. Seeing that his cavalry would not be able to maneuver on the steep, rocky ground, he relied on the infantry. On his right wing he placed his shield-bearing guards and the foot Companions, an elite Macedonian infantry unit much like the Companion cavalry. The Companion foot stretched to the left wing. In front of the right wing, Alexander placed the archers and the Agrianians, who were foot soldiers. In front of the left wing he stationed Thracian javelin throwers. Some Termessians had left their city and came to aid their fellow Pisidians at Sagalassus.

Alexander attacked, leading with the right wing. The archers fired their volleys and then fell back, but the Agrianians held their ground. Then the Macedonian phalanx came up, with Alexander in the lead. The Pisidians, our lost book tells us, wore no armor and so fell in large numbers and were routed. Here we hear a recurring refrain: the Pisidians retreated and, knowing the country well and being light of armor, made their escape. The soldiers in Alexander's army, on the other hand, had no knowledge of the land and were heavily armored and so didn't pursue with any zeal.

While it is perfectly logical and reasonable that this would have been the case, it is interesting that it is repeated so often in Arrian's account, and it seems quite likely that it is repeated in the same manner in Ptolemy's *History*. Thus we might consider that there is some need on Ptolemy's part to explain, after almost every battle, why Alexander's army did not pursue its enemy and why the enemy was able to make good its retreat. The need would seem to be a question of power. Why didn't Alexander stomp out his enemy completely? How could he let some of them get away from him? The answer is the ignorance of terrain and heavy armor, reasons that were understandable and legitimate, and not—what Ptolemy might be afraid people might conclude—that there was any fear on the part of the Macedonians.

Having taken the city of Sagalassus, Alexander was able to easily conquer the rest of Pisidia, including Termessus. He then moved farther north to Phrygia, in central Anatolia. After a few days of marching, Alexander arrived at Celaenae, another well-fortified city on a hill. Alexander received emissaries from the city saying they would surrender the city to him on a given date if he could just wait until that day. Alexander, again not wanting to spend a long time besieging the city, agreed and left a contingent of fifteen hundred troops to face the eleven hundred troops stationed in the city. He declared Antigonus One-Eyed, a Macedonian commander who had served under Philip II, viceroy over all of Phrygia. With this presumptuous proclamation, he marched toward Gordium.

Alexander's various forces converged at or near Gordium, the legendary seat of the kings of Phrygia, the best known of these being Midas. It seems likely that our lost book is the source for the military maneuvers at this point. Arrian states that Parmenion's force, which had been detached and had been subduing the area, rejoined Alexander's force. The newly married men who had been allowed to leave for what is presumed to have been a few months now returned to Gordium, along with the new soldiers they had been encouraged to recruit. It was at this point that Alexander went to the local temple of Zeus and found the cart tied with the knot associated with the Gordian Knot. The following story comes from Arrian:

Gordius had been a poor farmer with only two oxen to his name. One was for his cart and the other for his plow. One day an eagle settled on his yoke while he was plowing. The eagle remained there for the rest of the day, only leaving when the work of plowing had been finished. Seeing this as an omen of some kind, Gordius went to Telmissus, known to be the home of many seers. (That must have been true even in Alexander's day because he consulted a soothsayer from Telmissus at least once.) At Telmissus, Gordius found a girl and told her the story of the eagle. She, being from a family of seers, advised him to make sacrifices to Zeus at the place he had seen the eagle. Gordius persuaded the girl to go with him to ensure he conducted the sacrifices properly. The two ended up marrying, and they had a son named Midas.

The region of Phrygia, in the meantime, had fallen into civil war and was in a most awful state of chaos. An oracle had been called on, and this oracle said that a wagon would bring them their new king, and he would put an end to their civil war. The Phrygians were discussing what this could mean when Midas, along with his father and mother, drove their wagon into the city of Gordium, and so the Phrygians declared Midas their king, and he did end their war. In honor of Zeus, Midas had his father's wagon displayed in the temple and arranged for it to be tied with a knot of peculiar complexity. A legend arose around this knot that whoever was able to untie it would become master of Asia, or master of the world. In other stories, Gordius was the first king, and he founded the city of Gordium, having the knot tied on his wagon in the acropolis.

Because this is a legend of ancient Anatolia passed to us from the Greeks through the Roman era via multiple sources, it seems reasonable to think that some of it is fabricated. Still, we can see an outline of the legend that Alexander would have heard and we can come to some logical conclusions based on what we know. First, it seems all but certain that there was a cart and a complex knot in the temple of Zeus when Alexander came there because Arrian and Curtius refer to him dealing with the knot. We are told that Alexander had an impulse to go to the temple and see this cart. It seems certain that some sort of legend had grown around the cart and the knot that tied it. We don't know exactly what the prize was for untying the knot—mastery of Asia, control of the world, perhaps just control over Phrygia. Alexander saw in this knot the potential to further cement his living legend, to gain support and weaken opposition. Fulfilling a prophecy is great for public relations.

Arrian and Plutarch agree on Aristobulus's version of what Alexander did when he came to the temple and found the cart (Plutarch says it was a chariot) tied to a pole. Arrian says, "But Aristobulus tells us it was easy for him to undo it, by only pulling the pin out of the pole, to which the yoke was tied, and afterwards drawing off the yoke itself from below." The third book of Quintus Curtius Rufus's *The History of Alexander* (the first two books are lost) picks up near Gordium: "For some time Alexander wrestled unsuccessfully with the hidden knots. Then he said: 'It makes no difference how they're untied,' and cut through all the thongs with his sword, thus evading the oracle's prophecy—or, indeed, fulfilling it." Plutarch and Arrian acknowledge this version of the "untying" of the knot as one given by other writers. The question remains, what did Ptolemy's *History* have to say about the famous Gordian Knot?

It is interesting that Arrian points out what Aristobulus said and then simply states that "according to some," Alexander cut through the cornel-wood rope but does not specify what Ptolemy said on the subject. This leads us to two possible conclusions: Ptolemy's report agreed with other sources that Alexander simply cut the rope, or Ptolemy simply didn't mention the scene in Gordium. If Ptolemy had said that Alexander cut the rope, it seems likely that Arrian would have mentioned that, but if he ignored it, then it seems reasonable that Arrian wouldn't feel compelled to mention that Ptolemy was silent. For instance, Diodorus doesn't mention the Gordian Knot, so it seems likely it might not have been as famous a story as it would eventually come to be. Ptolemy might not have been at the temple that day, or he might have forgotten about it by the time he wrote his *History*. As always, we can say nothing for certain, but the most reasonable explanation is that our lost book doesn't mention the Gordian Knot.

While this was going on, the Persian general Memnon was contriving to take the war to Macedon and Greece. Having been given command of the whole Persian fleet by Darius, he assembled a large body of ships and captured Chios, an island off the coast of modern-day Turkey. He then went on to the island of Lesbos, where he engaged in an assault against the people there. This is when he caught an unknown illness and died. Memnon's death was of the utmost strategic importance. By all accounts, Memnon was a competent leader, and his death meant the loss of a great commander and the need for a sudden shift in Persian leadership. The immediate command was passed on to Memnon's nephew Pharnabazus, who continued the attack on Lesbos. The Persians won that island but were forestalled by a small fleet put together under the orders of Antipater, the ruler of Macedon in Alexander's absence.

Meanwhile, Alexander left Gordium and Phrygia and entered Cappadocia. This region lies at the eastern end of Anatolia and is particularly significant because our main source for the lost book, Arrian, was governor of this land during the second century AD. This means that Arrian could have spent a great deal of time in his *Anabasis* describing the geography and people of Cappadocia, but he does not. This is a clear indication that he is remaining strict in his adherence to the historical tale of Alexander and his primary focus on military exploits. This echoes our lost book, and some historians have even suggested that Arrian's account is basically a rewrite of Ptolemy's *History.* I would not take it to that extreme, but I feel it is at moments, more often than Arrian is willing to cite, a copy of the lost book.

Alexander did not remain in Cappadocia long; he conquered most of the land and left a man named Sabictas as satrap of the region. From there he traveled south into Cilicia, and coming to the Cilician Gates, he found them well defended. The gates are, in fact, a natural pass between two ridges. It has been said that before the pass was widened by artillery blasts, it was only wide enough for one loaded camel to pass through at a time. Our lost book would tell us that Alexander saw the obvious flaw with a straightforward assault on the pass and so left Parmenion with some troops to camp near the gates while he took a selection of soldiers to approach the defenders of the pass by the cover of night. Alexander's approach was detected, but the end result was still what he hoped for. The somewhat-surprise attack caused the defenders to be routed, and Alexander controlled the pass.

Alexander then captured the city of Tarsus, and at this point he fell ill. Arrian says that Aristobulus blamed exhaustion, while "others say that Alexander, sweaty and overcome by heat, had wanted a bath and had dived into the river Cyndus for a swim (the Cyndus runs right through the city of Tarsus, and with its springs in the Taurus mountains and a course through open country its water is cold and clear)." As with the tale of the Gordian Knot, we are told what Aristobulus cited as the cause of Alexander's illness but not, specifically, what Ptolemy claimed. But here the circumstances are a bit different. Knowing that Arrian's main source is Ptolemy, it seems possible that the account that follows about Alexander's illness comes directly from the *History.* Unlike the stories about the Gordian Knot, which disagree on Alexander's actions, the only thing that Arrian's sources seem to disagree on is the cause of his illness.

Alexander's doctors seemed to think he was on the verge of death—all except Philip of Acarnania, who believed Alexander simply needed a purgative or laxative. Philip was in the middle of mixing up Alexander's draught when Alexander was handed a letter from Parmenion saying that Philip could not be trusted and that he had been bribed by Darius to poison the Macedonian king. Alexander took the draught from Philip and handed the note to the doctor. He drank down the medicine while Philip read the note. The doctor assured him that he was in no danger, and Alexander showed that he trusted his friends and was not so easily led to suspicion. The medicine had its effect, and Alexander recovered from his illness. Once again, Parmenion was proven wrongly fretful and perhaps a little foolish. One almost begins to feel some sympathy for the man. He tries to do right by the king but is so often disregarded and proven wrong that one wonders if he had any success in life, or if this is all just propaganda against him.

Yet Parmenion remained Alexander's assumed second in command and was immediately tasked by the king to hold the pass that led from Cilicia into Assyrian territory and thus to forestall any advance by the enemy that way. Alexander then went to Anchialus, and then to Soli, where he established a garrison and fined the people two hundred talents for being pro-Persian. He then took a force and for seven days fought and defeated some of the Cilicians holding the mountains in the area. Then he went back to Soli. There he learned that Asander, nephew to Parmenion, and Ptolemy (most likely not the author of the lost book but another commander of the same name) had defeated the Persian Orontobates in a great battle that saw Persian casualties at seven hundred infantry and fifty cavalry, along with one thousand prisoners captured. It is highly likely that this account and these figures come from the lost book. This defeat of Orontobates added to Alexander's conquests, which now included the citadel of Halicarnassus, Myndus, Caunus, Thera, Callipolis, Cos, and Triopium.

Arrian, here likely echoing Ptolemy's *History*, tells us, "In Soli Alexander offered sacrifice to Asclepius [god of medical arts], conducting a procession of the entire army, celebrating a torch race, and superintending a gymnastic and musical contest." As long as Ptolemy was in the area (and there is no reason to believe he was not), then he was surely at these exhibitions and games. Alexander was probably celebrating the victory of Orontobates, his recent victories in Cilicia and Cappadocia, as well as his over-coming of a serious illness, hence the attention to Asclepius.

From Soli he went to Magarsus and then to Mallus. There he imprisoned citizens breeding revolution among the people and remitted the tribute the Mallotes had been paying to the Persians. His reason for this, we are told by our lost book, was that Mallus was a colony of the Argives', from Argos, and Alexander was descended from the Argives, who were descended from the Greek hero Heracles. Thus Alexander considered these people kin of a kind and so did not wish to see them burdened with a tribute.

five

BATTLING DARIUS

I T WAS NOW NOVEMBER 333 BC. DARIUS HAD NOT BEEN IDLE while Alexander campaigned through Anatolia. In fact, he had amassed a huge army and was determined to bring down this upstart king from Macedon. He had convened his army as early as late summer and was awaiting Alexander in a place called Sochoi in the northern Syrian plains. This was an ideal spot for him to maneuver his large army. Estimates range greatly on the numbers of the Persian force. Arrian and Plutarch give us an estimate of six hundred thousand, which is almost certainly a gross overestimate. It is assumed they drew from the same source, which may have been our lost book. A more likely modern estimate would be about one hundred thousand, which, by the standards of the day, was truly massive.

Darius did not remain in Sochoi, however. Modern scholars offer a wide range of reasons for this. Ptolemy's *History* probably gave what is considered the traditional reason, that Darius grew impatient waiting for Alexander, who had taken a long time recovering from his illness and had taken time to conquer places in Cilicia before coming into Syria. One must question, as well,

Alexander's motives for seeming to delay meeting Darius. Perhaps, as some have argued, it was that Alexander lacked information on the Persian army's location and condition. Perhaps he hoped to lure Darius into the more mountainous and narrow regions north of the Syrian plains. Perhaps Darius had been informed that Alexander was sick or that he had divided his force, which he did, and hoped to capitalize on these events by attacking Alexander swiftly.

Our lost book probably echoes the official history of Callisthenes, which is relayed in Arrian's account. Darius became convinced by the flatterers of his court that Alexander did not desire to go any farther in his conquest, and that the Macedonians would stop in Cilicia and use the strong mountains that lie to the southeast as their natural border. These men convinced the Persian king that Alexander had learned that Darius had taken the field against him and had grown afraid and did not want to risk a war with the great Persian host. However, a Greek deserter named Amyntas (not the general of the same name) stated with confidence that Alexander would meet Darius wherever the king might be and so it was best to stay in Sochoi where the flat, open land was most advantageous for Darius's large force and chariots.

Curtius Rufus breaks down Darius's forces as follows: one hundred thousand Persians, sixty thousand Medes, twelve thousand Barcanian warriors, forty-seven thousand Armenians, six thousand Hyrcanian horsemen, one thousand Tapurian cavalry, forty thousand Derbices, thirty thousand Greek mercenaries, and a few thousand miscellaneous soldiers. As previously noted, such numbers are almost certainly highly inflated. What they do show is that Darius commanded a large and varied force. Alexander's army at this time was probably close to forty thousand.

Our lost book would probably tell us that Darius left the plains and headed through the Amanic Gates, which lie to the north of Issus and the Gulf of Issus, just at the place where

Anatolia becomes Syria. Alexander was heading in a southeasterly direction that passed through Issus and came to the Syrian Gates, which is sometimes identified as the Pillar of Jonah, a narrow, natural passage. This brought Darius up to Alexander's rear and cut off Alexander's support and communication lines. Arrian and other sources tell us that when Darius came to Issus, he found many of Alexander's sick soldiers who had been left behind. These soldiers were maimed and killed, presumably upon Darius's orders. Alexander did not at first believe that Darius was at his rear, so he sent a contingent of Companions in a boat into the Gulf of Issus to determine if the massive Persian army was truly there. They soon returned to confirm the reports.

Alexander called his generals and commanders to him. Ptolemy would have been there, one of the many familiar faces, hearing Alexander's words. They had already faced much together, and now they would face more. They had already beaten Persian forces at Granicus; Alexander assured them that they would succeed again. They were fighting in a place of narrow mountain passes, ideally suited for Alexander's smaller, mobile force. Alexander criticized the Persians and Medes, saying they had grown soft from easy living while the Greeks were a hard and warlike people. It would be a battle of free men against slaves, he told them, and the scales were obviously in their favor. They had Alexander to lead them, while the Persians had only Darius. Their reward would be the whole of Asia, to rule over as they saw fit.

No doubt the commanders envisioned the honor and power that awaited them. They would be able to become lords of vast tracts of land because they would have been by Alexander's side in this victory. But many of them were probably doubtful of the outcome of such a contest, even if they didn't show it to their fellows. The Persians had them vastly outnumbered, cut off from their supply lines, and benefited from home-field advantage.

Alexander moved his army back toward Issus and by midnight controlled the Syrian Gates. Then he rested his troops for a few hours. By dawn he ordered his men to march west, through the Syrian Gates, with the ridge to their right and the sea to their left. The gates were passed, and Alexander broadened his line. Eventually his men were in fighting formation as follows: on the far right wing, close to the ridge, were the royal guard and foot guards under Nicanor, son of Parmenion, and next to them were Coenus's brigade and Perdiccas's brigade. On the left wing was the general Amyntas's brigade; then the brigade of Ptolemy, son of Seleucus and a Macedonian commander not to be confused with our author; then Meleager's brigade. Parmenion had command of all the forces on the left wing, with Alexander presumably commanding the right. The Companion cavalry and Thessalian cavalry joined Alexander on the right, while the Peloponnesians and other cavalry went to the left. These arrangements all come from Arrian, and it is very probable that he took them directly from Ptolemy's account.

Darius arranged most of his infantry to the center and left, while most of the cavalry went to his right, facing Alexander's left. Seeing this to be the case, Alexander called for the Thessalian cavalry to immediately go to the left wing. He sent some archers to the right. A group of Persians had taken to the ridge to his right and threatened to flank him on that side, so he sent a force of Agrianians and archers to uproot them. This was accomplished, and he needed to leave only a small force to defend the ridge. Darius's forces were aligned and standing still at the edge of the Pinarus River that separated the two armies. Alexander advanced.

He called on his men to be brave, and his men answered back with a cheer. They advanced at walking pace until they were within range of the Persian archers. Alexander and his company on the right rushed forward and surprised the enemy with the speed of their assault. The Persian left wing began to give way under this sudden assault, and the archers were not able to

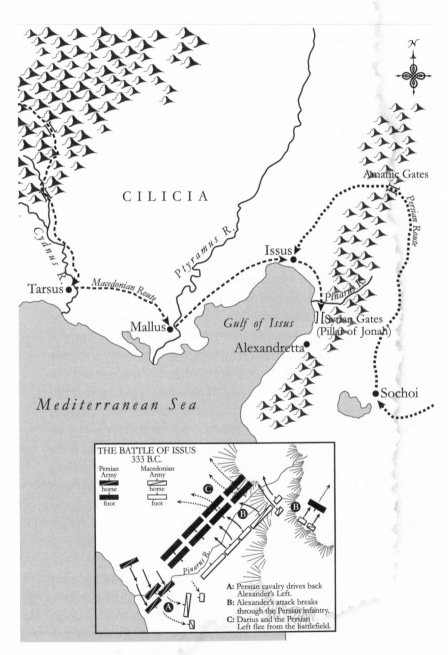

Map 2. The Battle of Issus, 333 B.C.

inflict much damage. The center of Alexander's forces faced the Greek mercenaries and did not attack with as much speed, so they were not able to push back the Persian forces in the same way the right had. Here Ptolemy, son of Seleucus, died in the battle.

The right wing, being victorious in its effort, swung around to help in the attack of the center. As Arrian echoes our lost book, "They first drove them back from the river, then, outflanking the now broken section of the Persian army, charged into the mercenaries from the side and began cutting them down." At the same time, the Persian cavalry had advanced across the river and given hard battle to Parmenion's forces. It might have had a small victory in its corner of the battle if it had not realized that the Persian center and left had fallen, leaving it alone on the field. Thus the Persian right was routed, and the entire force retreated. The Persians and Darius had been defeated.

Darius, it would later be claimed, fled as soon as his left wing was beaten back by Alexander. It is hard to verify the truth in this report. It seems almost certain that this is what Ptolemy would record in his *History*, but how could he have known the moment of Darius's flight? Perhaps Darius did pull back when his left wing collapsed; perhaps he fled when he saw the Greek mercenaries destroyed. All that can be said for certain is that at some point, Darius thought it prudent to flee. He must have known that if Alexander captured or killed him, the defeat would have been total. The victors might portray his fleeing as cowardice, but it is likely that Darius saw it as his and the Persians best option under the circumstances. If the roles were reversed and Alexander saw his army begin to crumble that day, what would he have done?

What is not in question is that this was a great victory for Alexander and that he still wished to capture Darius if possible. Thus he pursued the Persian king, who had abandoned his chariot and was riding on horseback to escape. But Darius had a head start on Alexander, and once night fell, it was deemed impossible to pursue him. Alexander claimed Darius's chariot, shield, robe, and bow as prizes.

The dead were great in number. Directly from our lost book comes the account that Ptolemy, who indicated he was with Alexander at the time, came upon a ravine in the pursuit of Darius (it is not clear where this was). It was possible to cross the ravine without touching the ground by walking over the bodies piled there. The number given for the dead overall is one hundred thousand, which seems implausible, but it must have been more than anyone had ever seen. Like the world wars thousands of years in the future, the battlefield would have been covered with corpses. Stretching from the ridges of the Amanus Mountains to the Gulf of Issus, as far as the eye could see lay men killed by sword and lance, shot with arrows or javelins, or trampled by horses.

The detail from Ptolemy's *History* about the bodies in the ravine is not just gruesome but also telling about what our lost book would have covered. It would appear from this section that Ptolemy recorded personal anecdotes in the lost book. This leads us to wonder if the book read more like a memoir than a history, or perhaps something in between. There would have been details concerning the arrangements of troops, but also tales from the battlefield; personal accounts of what Ptolemy saw and took part in.

Darius might have escaped Issus, but his wife, mother, daughters, and infant son did not. They were captured by the Macedonians immediately after the battle had been won. Besides the loss of his army, this might have been the greater blow to Darius. By Arrian's account, and thus we can venture to presume Ptolemy's account, Alexander treated Darius's family well. At first, Darius's mother, wife, and children were distraught with grief, thinking Darius had died. Alexander sent them a messenger to tell them Darius still lived. Curtius Rufus indicates the women were also under the impression that they were to be executed. The messenger told them this was not the case, that

Alexander wished them to live. Furthermore, he afforded them the same luxuries they had been accustomed to and would not tolerate their being exposed to anything unseemly (which, in a camp of soldiers newly victorious, must have been difficult). Ptolemy and Aristobulus agree that Alexander's motives for this were quite plain. He let Darius's family retain all the things befitting their royal rank, and even let his wife and mother continue to be called queens, "for he had not undertaken the war against Darius from a feeling of hatred, but he had conducted it in a legitimate manner for the empire of Asia." Here again we see Ptolemy presenting Alexander as the rational imperialist. He was not, it would seem, seeking to avenge anything but merely to add to his dominion.

Next we move beyond Alexander's army. If Ptolemy reported this information, it would have been something he obtained after the fact, gleaned from other sources. First we are told that Darius fled quickly east and put the Euphrates River between himself and Alexander. He gathered those who had escaped the battle and set his sights on once again amassing an army. Amyntas, the Macedonian deserter, along with other Greek deserters had about eight thousand troops and fled south and east, eventually settling in Egypt. There Amyntas fell afoul of the locals and was killed. Pharnabazus and Autophradates still commanded what remained of Memnon's fleet at Chios. They dispatched ships to Cos and to Halicarnassus, in the hopes of returning that city to Persian control. They were met by Agis, the king of the Spartans, who asked for money and a force of soldiers so he could make war in the Peloponnesus against the Greeks loyal to Alexander. By this time news had reached them of Alexander's victory at Issus so they changed their plans. Agis went to Halicarnassus with Autophradates while sending some ships to Crete to win over that island. Pharnabazus returned to the islands the Persian fleet had already conquered in the hopes of stopping any revolts since the news of Issus might turn out to be incendiary.

Alexander traveled farther into Syria, and here he is reported to have received a letter from Darius. According to the Roman writer Diodorus, Darius "wrote to Alexander advising him to bear his success as one who was only human and to release the captives in return for a large ransom. He added that he would yield to Alexander the territory and cities of Asia west of the Halys River if he would sign a treaty of friendship with him." Diodorus then claims that Alexander hid this letter from his advisers and presented one that was more likely to get the reaction he wanted. In Arrian's telling, which may have been taken from Ptolemy's *History,* there is no mention of Darius offering all of Anatolia to Alexander. Since we don't know Diodorus's source, we can't say for certain what Darius's letter actually said and if there truly was such an offer on the table. It seems plausible that our lost book doesn't make mention of any such offer since it does not show up in Arrian's account.

According to Arrian, Alexander replied to Darius, "Your ancestors came into Macedon and the rest of Greece and treated us ill, without any previous injury from us. I, having been appointed commander-in-chief of the Greeks, and wishing to take revenge on the Persians, crossed into Asia, hostilities being begun by you." Alexander's motivation of revenge would have sounded like a hollow pretense even in Ptolemy's *History.* If Alexander had sought revenge, he would have treated his prisoners differently and he wouldn't have given the respect and honor he did to Darius's family.

Why did he not tell Darius that he was simply a king looking to expand his kingdom and that the Persian Empire was a prize too great to ignore? Because, I think, Alexander's pretense was partly true, or at least it was true when it was most convenient. Alexander did see himself as representative of the Greeks, but he was also a king expanding an empire. Thus he punished the Persians when he deemed appropriate, for instance, laying fines on cities for being too supportive of Persian rule. But he also saved cities from destruction and installed garrisons and viceroys to rule and maintain order. He knew that for the Greeks in his army, the Persians were ancient enemies. So he had to maintain a position of revenge against the Persian barbarians, but he also had designs to conquer as much as he could and make it all part of his kingdom. His ambitions were grandiose; his motivations were varied. His intended audience for his letter was not just Darius but his own army. He blamed the death of his father, Philip, on Darius. He accused Darius of treating his people unjustly and of trying to incite other Greeks to war against Alexander and offering money to them, stating that only the Spartans accepted.

In his letter, he seemed to possibly acknowledge an offer of territory by Darius, stating that he had, by being victorious in battle, come into possession of Darius's land. He invited Darius to approach him as lord of Asia and then to ask for his family. Alexander insinuated that he would give Darius his family if Darius came to him in person, acknowledging him as lord of Asia. If Darius would not do this, then Alexander suggested he prepare for another battle and implored him to not run away.

How can we know if the words of these letters carry any truth? Were copies made of the letters? Did someone, maybe Ptolemy, keep a copy and then, decades after the fact, take them out and copy them down verbatim? Is there any truth in Diodorus's assertion that Alexander kept the real letter from Darius a secret from his generals and advisers? We'll probably never know, but it does seem possible that there was an exchange of letters between the two kings. The exact nature of these letters is perhaps unknowable, but we can be sure that Darius sought to come to some agreement with Alexander, a way to end the war. And we can be equally certain that Alexander refused any such compromise. Alexander, as he said in his letter, wanted to be lord of Asia, nothing else would do.

Alexander had sent Parmenion to Damascus with a contingent of cavalry in order to secure a vast treasure that Darius had sent there before the battle at Issus. Parmenion had succeeded in capturing this horde, though there seems to be some indication that someone (either acting by direction of Darius or hoping to steal the treasure themselves) had managed to get it out of Damascus. Parmenion tracked it down and returned it to the city. There he also captured four Greek ambassadors who had been sent to treat with Darius. They were Euthycles the Spartan; Thessaliscus and Dionysodorus, both from Thebes; and Iphicrates from Athens. Dionysodorus was an Olympic victor, and Iphicrates was the son of the general Iphicrates. These ambassadors were taken to Alexander.

When the king met them he immediately released Thessaliscus and Dionysodorus, for a number of reasons. First, he said their actions were understandable since their home had been destroyed and their people enslaved by the Macedonians, and he felt compassion for them because of this. Also, he said that Thessaliscus came from a distinguished family and Dionysodorus was an Olympic victor, and so he felt they deserved their freedom. It was said that because of his love for Athens, Alexander not only freed Iphicrates but allowed him to join his retinue. The ambassador stayed with Alexander until Iphicrates died and the king sent his bones back to Athens. Alexander was less inclined to be merciful to Euthycles since the Spartans had always been openly hostile toward the Macedonians and Alexander. At first he kept him under guard as a prisoner, but eventually he freed him. Here again we see an Alexander who is just and compassionate. One must remember a few things that might temper this view of Alexander.

First, he was fresh off a great victory. There were reports that he had suffered a serious wound on his thigh during the battle, but it is obvious that this didn't deter him in conducting his pursuit of Darius or treating with Darius's family. He is riding high on this victory. Sparing the lives of a few Greek ambassadors would cost him very little.

Also, the Thebans were of no real threat to him; he had already made sure of that by destroying their city. He obviously felt no real threat from Athens and perhaps believed that sparing their ambassador to Darius would be a reason for them to hold him in higher esteem. His treatment of the Spartan was a little more understandable. He doesn't appear to have been cruel, but he kept the man as a prisoner for some time, releasing him, as Arrian tells us, "as his [Alexander's] successes began to multiply." This again indicates a link between Alexander's victories and his magnanimity.

Alexander marched south into Syria. He took Byblus and Sidon without any bloodshed, the inhabitants agreeing to terms of surrender and, in the case of Sidon, inviting Alexander into their city as a liberator, since they had no love for Persians. From here he headed toward Tyre, the great coastal city and trading center. Tyre sent envoys to say the city would follow whatever orders Alexander gave. Alexander told them he intended to come into the city so he could sacrifice to Heracles.

six

THE SIEGE OF TYRE

TYRE IS A CITY WITH A LONG AND ILLUSTRIOUS HISTORY. Originally it was Phoenician, and its people were among the first to navigate the waters of the Mediterranean Sea. Tyre became a great trading port, and from its harbor left people who established colonies throughout the Mediterranean, including Carthage in northern Africa, islands in the Aegean, Sicily, Corsica, and even in Spain. The city consisted of two parts: a fortress on the mainland called "Old Tyre" and the city itself, which existed on a rocky island half a mile from the shore, which was a very defendable location. A story says the city was besieged by the Assyrian Shalmaneser for five years and later by the Babylonian Nebuchadnezzar for thirteen years, both without apparent success.

Within the island city there was an ancient temple to Heracles. Arrian gives a somewhat long-winded explanation of the origins of the temple and the Tyrian Heracles that can be summarized by saying that the Tyrians worshipped a different Heracles than others in Greece and that Alexander wished to go to the Tyrian Heracles and sacrifice in the Tyrian way to their god. He had done similar things at previous temples and sacred

sites he had visited, and this seems in line with his public relations campaign of winning over locals by observing their religious rites. The Tyrians stated they would follow any orders
from Alexander but they would not allow any Macedonians or
Persians into their city. This seemed to be the safest strategy, as
they must have been unsure of the outcome of the war. Thus,
Alexander could not enter the city and sacrifice to Heracles at
his temple. Alexander was angered by this response and called
together his Companions, including Ptolemy, and other army
leaders. Then, according to Arrian, he delivered a speech to
them on their current situation:

> Friends and allies, I see two threats to our security. An advance
> on Egypt is not safe as long as the Persians control the sea. And
> the pursuit of Darius is not safe either if we leave behind us
> ambiguity in Tyre itself with Egypt and Cyprus still held by the
> Persians. This has particular relevance to the situation in
> Greece. The Persians could regain control of the seaboard if we
> have taken our full force on an offensive against Babylon and
> Darius: they could then augment their fleet and carry war to
> Greece, where the Spartans are in open conflict with us and our
> hold on Athens is secured at the present more by fear than sym-
> pathy. But with Tyre destroyed the whole of Phoenicia would be
> in our hands, and the Phoenician navy, which forms the largest
> and the strongest part of the Persian fleet, would in all likeli-
> hood come over to us—when their cities are in our control the
> Phoenician rowers and marines will not want to put themselves
> at risk in the service of others.

He went on to say that Cyprus would need little persuasion
to side with them or would fall easily to a naval attack after the
taking of Tyre. He theorized that with the Macedonian and
Phoenician fleets combined, and with Cyprus on their side, they
would then have command of the sea. This would clear the way
for an expedition to Egypt. Upon gaining control in Egypt,
there would be no more worries of an attack on Greece and so
they could then make their move on Babylon.

This shows that Alexander had good intelligence on his enemy, understood the threat that the Persian fleet continued to pose, and knew that the Spartans had allied themselves with the Persians. He read the situation carefully and proposed a sound strategy to ensure total victory over the enemy. Here again we see an Alexander who doesn't consult with anyone but simply delivers his reasons and plans, and everyone gathered can do nothing but agree with such perfect sense. Had one of his commanders approached him before the speech and given him reasons to besiege Tyre? Had anyone needed to remind him of the Persian fleet or the actions of the Spartans? Had anyone needed to caution him against a direct pursuit of Darius? There's no mention of these things happening, but that doesn't mean they didn't. In Ptolemy's depiction of Alexander, he obviously tried to present the king as a glorious and great leader, and it might have seemed pointless or even antithetical to include any deliberations or arguments over strategy. In our lost book, Alexander alone determines most of the plans, and Alexander alone leads his army.

Next, Alexander determined exactly how they would besiege the island city: they would build a mole, or causeway, from Old Tyre on the mainland to the island and bring their siege engines right to the city walls. The building of the mole was a massive undertaking. Today Tyre is no longer a city island but is connected to the mainland by a wide, natural stretch of land; if this had been the case in 332 BC, the siege would not have involved as much labor as it did. Arrian, here probably referencing Aristobulus (as it is believed he was an engineer for Alexander's army), tells us that the mole was built primarily with wood and stone. The men laid the stones down first and then piled the wood on top of them. It seems likely, though Arrian doesn't mention it, that they then put some earth over the wood, making a road they could bring the siege engines across. The strait of water they were crossing was shallow near the mainland but deepened greatly the closer they got to the city. Arrian gives the deepest point to be three fathoms, or roughly eighteen feet deep.

As they came close to the city, the soldiers-turned-builders came under many difficulties. The depth of the water made the endeavor that much harder, plus they faced strong winds that consistently battered them. Worse still was the fact that they were now within range of Tyrian missiles and so could be fired on while they worked. Imagine building a road while javelins and flaming arrows are raining down on you. In response, Alexander's army built two towers at the end of the mole with catapults situated at the tops; the towers were covered with skins and hides to prevent them from catching fire as easily as exposed wood and to afford protection to those inside the towers. The Tyrians regularly sent out boats to harass the Macedonians. These boats were turned back by missiles fired from the newly constructed towers.

The Tyrians resolved to destroy the towers. They took a horse-transport boat and loaded the stern of the ship so the prow stuck out of the water. They piled in the boat any tinder they could find and covered it in pitch and sulfur and anything else that would burn. Across the two masts they suspended cauldrons of various fuels that would feed the flames once they spilled onto the fire below. They brought out boats to tow this laden vessel toward the towers at the end of the mole. They lighted their fires just when they were coming close, and the engulfed boat landed just below the towers. The masts burned and broke, and the fuel from the cauldrons fell onto the fire and made it grow even higher, igniting the towers, the skins and hides proving insufficient to stop the fire. While this was happening, the Tyrians kept up a steady barrage of arrows from their ships so that Alexander's army couldn't attempt to put out the fires. The towers were destroyed, and Alexander realized that he needed to adjust his strategy. As long as the Tyrians controlled the sea, his siege would be unsuccessful.

Alexander took some of his troops and marched back to Sidon with the hope of assembling any fleet he could muster there. At this moment, like so many others, fortune smiled on

Alexander and his cause. For it was then that Gerostratus, king of Aradus, and Enylus, king of Byblus, deserted from Autophradates and his Persian fleet and brought their triremes, along with those from Sidon, to Alexander's side, because their respective cities were now under Alexander's control. This resulted in about eighty ships coming to Alexander. Around the same time, nine triremes arrived from Rhodes together with the state trireme they called the Guard ship. Three ships arrived from Soli and Mallus, and ten from Lycia. A penteconter, a ship with fifty oarsmen, arrived from Macedon. As Arrian tells us, "Not long afterwards the kings of Cyprus also came into Sidon with some one hundred and twenty ships: they had heard of Darius's defeat at Issus, and it alarmed them that the whole of Phoenicia was now in Alexander's control." Alexander took all the ships and forgave any of the kings who had sided with the Persians. It is said he forgave them because he saw that what they did, they did out of necessity, and so he harbored no ill will toward them. But it must also be assumed that he was exceptionally grateful for this bounty of ships that he now had at his disposal.

While his siege engines were being built and his ships outfitted for the taking of Tyre, our lost book tells us that Alexander and a force of troops ventured into Arabia, where, in ten days, he subdued the whole region through conquest or capitulation and then returned to Sidon. It is hard to determine where exactly Alexander went and what he did in Arabia, but it seems unlikely that he subdued the entire area in just ten days. Just before his death, Alexander began plans to take the rest of Arabia and add it to his domain. Our lost book, and Alexander himself, was probably ignorant of how large Arabia was and how many people lived there, with much of it being cut off by huge swaths of desert.

From Sidon, Alexander put as many soldiers as he could onto the ships and sailed against Tyre. The Tyrians, on seeing the large fleet arrayed in battle formation, withdrew from the sea and blocked up the mouths of the harbors with ships. Tyre had two harbors, one that faced the north and was often called the Sidon Harbor and another that faced the south and was called the Egypt Harbor. The following day, Alexander ordered the Cypriots to take their contingent of ships, with Andromachus as admiral, and set up a blockade at the Sidon Harbor; he had the Phoenicians do the same thing at the Egypt Harbor.

Around this time the siege engines were finished, and Alexander brought them out on the mole and also on boats to be sailed against the city walls. Those walls are said to have been 150 feet high in some places, and from the tops, the Tyrians shot down on any boats that came within their range. Being aboard these ships must have been exceptionally dangerous. The men had to maneuver the boats in such a way that the catapults could aim at the walls, and all the while arrows rained down on them. While this happened, the Tyrians would send out covered boats or divers who would cut anchor lines and send the ships adrift, preventing them from holding to any one position. It must have seemed an impossible task.

But Alexander's fleet solved one of those problems quickly by using chain for anchors instead of rope. Thus the divers and covered boats were thwarted. The fleet covered its own boats and managed to pull away some large rocks that had been dropped into the ocean to impede any boat from getting too close to the walls. Thus the Macedonians were able to convince the Tyrians that the walls would soon be conquered and their city was in imminent peril. Hoping to change the course of the siege, the Tyrians struck out to attack the Cypriot fleet blocking the Sidon Harbor. At first they came on in single file, slowly. When they were close, the Tyrians let out a shout and fiercely attacked the Cypriot ships, which were caught unawares. The Tyrians were successful in this first assault, sinking some ships and driving others ashore. Once Alexander became aware of this attack, he ordered as many ships as he could muster around the city in a counterattack. Once the Tyrians in the city became aware of the mass of ships bearing down on their fellows in the Sidon Harbor, they began to yell to their ships to return, but without success. They then used some sort of signs to draw the ships back, but it was too late for most of them. They were attacked by Alexander's fleet and destroyed or captured.

It is hard to say where Ptolemy was during this siege. There is no indication that he had any experience with sailing, nor is it believed he was an engineer building siege weapons. He would have most likely taken a backseat in this expedition, perhaps remaining on the mainland with the rest of the army, but it is likely that he was often near Alexander, as were the other Companions. Much of the army was still working on the mole, which eventually reached the island. Alexander had siege engines brought up to the mole and onto ships up to the city walls but was unable to break through the wall. He tried again toward the Sidon Harbor and was unsuccessful there. He tried again near the Egypt Harbor and broke through the wall, but the Tyrians were able to fight the Macedonians back.

The next day, Alexander ordered a coordinated, full-scale assault on the city. First siege engines were brought on ships and were able to take down part of the city wall. Then boats with bridges came to the opening and allowed foot soldiers to cross from the water into the city. Alexander, with the shield-bearing guards, attempted to scale the wall in a spot where it looked possible. At the same time, ships sailed into the harbors to harass the Tyrians there while they were busy defending the opening in their city walls. All the while, boats with siege engines and archers encircled the city where they could and fired into it so that the Tyrians might not be sure where they needed to defend. Admetus, the commander of the foot soldiers, was the first to mount the wall, but he was struck with a spear and died on the spot. The Macedonians gained a firm footing, however, and easily broke into the city. Next, Alexander and his Companions went through the wall and entered the city they had laid siege to for seven months.

The fighting inside the city was fierce. The Tyrians were fighting for their lives and for their city, and the Macedonians were fighting for their king and out of anger at this city that had resisted them for so long. Our lost book gives us a total of eight thousand Tyrians killed, while only four hundred Macedonians died in the siege and ensuing battle. As has been speculated with other totals, there is a chance the enemy's dead have been over-stated and Alexander's dead understated. It is said that some thirty thousand people—troops and citizens—were sold into slavery. However, sources outside our lost book claim that the Tyrians had sent at least some of their women, children, and eld-erly men to Carthage for safety before the siege began. Carthage was a colony of Tyre, and it is believed that the Tyrians might have held some hope that Carthage would come to their aid, but this never happened. Alexander finally came to the temple of Heracles, the place he had been denied by the Tyrians. Here he found several people seeking refuge, among them magistrates of the city, emissaries from Carthage, and the king of Tyre, Azemilcus. Alexander, perhaps flushed with victory, gave them amnesty. He sacrificed in the temple, as he had wanted to do seven months earlier. There he held a gymnastic contest, then held a torch race and a procession of his army in honor of Heracles, this all done in the blazing heat of July or August 332 BC. He dedicated the siege engine that brought down the wall of Tyre to the temple in honor of Heracles as well. Thus the siege of Tyre came to an end.

While the siege was still going, Arrian tells us, emissaries arrived from Darius. Diodorus puts their arrival later in Alexander's campaigns, but our lost book surely tells of them arriving while operations were being conducted to capture Tyre. The emissaries' offer was similar to the letter Darius had previ-ously written to Alexander. They offered a huge ransom for Darius's family, ten thousand talents; they offered half of Darius's kingdom; and they offered Darius's daughter in mar-riage to the Macedonian king. In exchange they asked only for peace and friendship with Alexander. Once again we are presented with a conversation between Parmenion and Alexander. Parmenion says that if he were Alexander, he would accept the Persian king's offer. Alexander replies that he would, too, if he were Parmenion. But because he is Alexander, he will not accept it. He had no need for Darius's money or his kingdom, for he would take the whole of both when he was finished, and if he wished to marry Darius's daughter he would, whether Darius wanted him to or not.

One must wonder if these conversations between Parmenion and Alexander come directly from Ptolemy's *History.* Since it has already been explained that Arrian calls Ptolemy his "main source," it is reasonable to suppose that these prominent conversations in Arrian come from our lost book. Ptolemy has good reason to cast Parmenion in a bad light, as we will see later. So was it truly just Parmenion being wrong and Alexander being right? As I have suggested before, there was probably a lively pro-and-con debate going on. Of Alexander's advisers, one side thought the king should accept Darius's terms, and the other side thought he should not. Who is to say what Parmenion actually said? Writing about it much later, Ptolemy knew which course the king would take, what Alexander's final decision would be. So he put into Alexander's mouth the words that degraded the side for peace and supported continuing the war with Persia. Ptolemy needed someone to cast against Alexander, and Parmenion was a perfect choice because he was Alexander's second in command and Ptolemy knew that Parmenion would come to an ignoble end. This explains the anti-Parmenion propaganda that seems to be so prevalent in our lost book.

Alexander then marched south and came to Gaza, the last city before entering Egypt. Today we think of Gaza as more of a region—the Gaza Strip—and it is, but there is also an ancient city within this region. Today it is the largest city in the Palestinian territories. In Alexander's time, it was also a large city, built on a "lofty mound," as Arrian calls it, with deep sand around it. Alexander commanded that siege engines be built so they could take the city. His engineers, perhaps with Aristobulus among them, argued that it couldn't be done. The mound was too steep, the walls too high. Alexander ordered them to build their own mound around the city, by means of which they could bring siege engines right up to the walls.

Having built the mole that stretched out to Tyre, Alexander's soldiers must have been well accustomed to manual labor of this kind. Still, Gaza is described as being on the edge of the desert. It almost doesn't matter what time of year it was, because it would have been hot and dusty work. Sand got into everything and clung to the soldiers' sweat-covered bodies.

They raised their artificial mound higher and higher, and all the while, the people of Gaza looked over their walls in wonder. The commander of Gaza was a Persian named Batis. He must have believed his city was impenetrable, as it rested on a steep mound with high, strong walls. Alexander did not believe all the walls were strong, and he had his builders focus on the southern walls, which were believed to be the weakest and easiest to destroy. Once the artificial mound was built, siege engines were moved into place before the southern walls. It is worth noting that the siege engines that Alexander employed, specifically the catapults, were new technology. His father, Philip, had been among the first commanders to use them effectively in the field.

Arrian tells us that "at this time while Alexander was offering sacrifice, and, crowned with garland, was about to commence the first sacred rite according to custom, a certain carnivorous bird, flying over the altar, let a stone which it was carrying with its claws fall upon his head. Alexander asked Aristander, the soothsayer, what this omen meant. He replied: 'O king, you will indeed capture the city, but you must take care of yourself this day.'" This indicated that Alexander would be in personal danger, which was not surprising since he was often in the front lines of combat.

This story probably comes from our lost book. It represents a common scene in Arrian, that of an omen or portent and the subsequent interpretation by one of the soothsayers Alexander appears to keep near him. These omens almost always involve birds, as these animals had important significance in Alexander's time, or dreams. For instance, before the taking of Tyre, Alexander is said to have dreamed that the god Heracles led the king by the hand into the city. This was interpreted by Aristander as a sign that he would, indeed, capture the city. Aristander was one of Alexander's most trusted soothsayers; as noted earlier, he predicted the plot to kill Alexander from the actions of a swallow. Thus our lost book shows us that Alexander was a firm believer in omens, or at least that he used them when it best suited him. Omens held power and could be used to show a god was on your side or was opposed to your enemy, things that might boost morale in your soldiers. According to Plutarch, when Alexander was at Tyre, Aristander claimed the city would be taken within the month by reading signs from a sacrifice. It was late in the month, and so Alexander simply officially changed the calendar to give him more time to take the city. Thus we see that omens could be worked around to benefit Alexander. In fact, Alexander seemed to use omens to legitimize his decisions, but he also disregarded them when they were not to his liking. Therefore, it is hard to come to any conclusions about Alexander's religious beliefs. He certainly observed religious rites, but mainly when it suited him to do so, so he could be seen as being favored by the gods. What he personally believed will most likely remain a mystery.

At first Alexander kept out of reach of the missiles the Gazans fired down on his men as they attempted to storm the city, but eventually he could hold himself back no longer. He entered the fray and was wounded by a bolt through the shoulder, thus fulfilling part of Aristander's prophecy that Alexander would be in personal danger. Alexander resolved to complete the rest. By this time, siege engines from Tyre had arrived, and Alexander had the artificial mound extended to encompass the whole city. Mines were dug under walls and towers, and they began to crumble. The Macedonians attacked once, twice, three times and were beaten back. The fourth time was the last needed. They scaled the wall on ladders and threw open the gates from the inside. Fierce fighting ensued in the streets of Gaza, and it is said that the Gazans fought to the last man, all dying in the battle. Alexander had the women and children sold into slavery. He repopulated the city with residents of the surrounding area.

A story that is most likely not in our lost book is how Alexander treated Batis, the Persian commander of the city. According to Curtius Rufus, Alexander had holes bored through Batis's legs and rings shoved through the openings, most likely between the bone and tendon of the lower leg. Then the man was tied to a chariot, which Alexander rode around the city, in imitation of Achilles's treatment of Hector at Troy. This act, if true, must have seemed unbecoming, and so Ptolemy avoided the subject entirely. It is interesting that Ptolemy seems to be fine with reporting that Alexander sold all the women and children of a city into slavery but perhaps shied away from showing Alexander dragging a man to death (or dragging a body, it is not clear) behind a chariot.

seven

EGYPT SURRENDERS

A T THIS POINT, ALEXANDER CROSSED INTO EGYPT. THERE would be no battles or sieges in the land of the pharaohs. The region was handed over to the Macedonians by the Persian governor of Egypt, Mazaces, who had already had word of the battle of Issus and the sieges of Tyre and Gaza and so saw no means or reason to fight Alexander's conquest. Alexander came to Pelusium, a city at the eastern edge of the Nile Delta. He installed a garrison and met up with his fleet, which he ordered to sail up the Nile to Memphis, the ancient capital of Egypt. He followed with his army and came to the city, where he sacrificed to the gods and held gymnastic and musical competitions, with artists and athletes coming all the way from Greece.

Gymnastics was a time-honored tradition in Greece, and Alexander's dedication to these competitions shows the Hellenization of his world. Here he is in Egypt, on the banks of the Nile, holding a very Greek competition with Greek participants. Greek education consisted of three parts: grammar, music, and gymnastics. Gymnastics was by far the most important of the three. Aristotle, Alexander's teacher, advised a fourth course of study: painting or drawing. Gymnastics, however, remained central to Greek life. The Greeks believed that a person could only have a healthy mind if he had a healthy body. To that end, people of all ages engaged in gymnastics, or exercising, and would go to the *gymnasia*. In Alexander's competitions, there would have been men who excelled in gymnastics. There would have been wrestling matches and swimming races, tugs-of-war and running. There might have been bare-knuckle boxing or pankration, which was a combination of wrestling and boxing and had barely any rules.

The musical competitions would have been a highly Greek affair as well. One of the key instruments would have been the autos, which was something like a double flute or recorder played with both hands on two separate pipes connected to a single mouthpiece. They would be made of reed stems, wood, or bone and produced a distinct and beautiful sound. Their music would have accompanied sacrifices, rituals, and theater. They helped keep time for oarsmen on triremes and were played at the gymnastic competitions. The other most common instrument would have been the lyre, specifically the cithara, which was a large concert lyre used especially in competitions and large gatherings. The music and feats of strength in Memphis would have had a festive air and perhaps made the soldiers feel almost like they were home and not on the other side of the Mediterranean, in a land of alien gods, customs, and people.

From Memphis, Alexander sailed down the river back toward the delta and there found the spot he thought perfect for a city. This would be the location of Alexandria. Arrian tells a story about the laying out of the city. "There is also a story told . . . ," he says, not attributing it to Ptolemy or Aristobulus, so we must assume that it likely comes from neither source. The story is that Alexander wanted to put down the layout of the city just as he wanted the engineers to build it, but there was nothing at hand to lay down the lines to mark the roads and buildings. Someone suggested using the barley meal that the soldiers carried, so this was used to mark the ground. Aristander, the eminent soothsayer, prophesied that this would mean the city would prosper primarily from the gifts of the earth. This would turn out to be true. If Ptolemy was with Alexander, which seems likely, he might have pondered the future of this city that Alexander was founding, but he could not have known that his future and the city were so greatly intertwined.

Around this time, Alexander decided to go to another temple, where a particularly well-known oracle existed. While this seems to be just another in a long line of journeys to temples for Alexander, this one would prove especially significant. The temple was to Ammon, a ram-headed god the Greeks associated with Zeus, and it could be found in Libya, across the desert to the west of Egypt. This was a perilous journey that Alexander proposed. Arrian speculates that Alexander might have already considered himself descended from Ammon. That is no stretch, because Alexander most certainly considered himself descended from Heracles, who was descended from Zeus.

According to Aristobulus, Alexander first went by way of the coast to Paraetonium, which was said to be roughly 180 miles away. Then he turned to the south and west into a sandy desert that held little water. Arrian reports that Alexander met with rain while crossing this desert, and so it was seen as a divine intervention. Though Curtius Rufus says the rain came only after Alexander and his men had become hopelessly thirsty, he also says that it may have simply come by chance and not at the hand of a god. Other sources say that at this point, a group of crows came into view and led the party to the oracle. Our lost book specifically states "two snakes went hissing in front of the army, and Alexander told his commanders to trust this divine sign and follow them: the snakes, Ptolemy says, led the way to the oracle and back again also." Arrian states that Aristobulus's account was that of the crows and agrees that this is the prevalent account, "but the precise truth of the matter is obscured by the conflicting accounts given by his historians."

Here we perceive two important things: one, Ptolemy differs in his account and attributes the divine hand coming in the form of snakes, and two, while Arrian admits that Aristobulus's crows are the more popular account, he will not concede to the more widely regarded version but holds Aristobulus and Ptolemy in equal measure and gives no credence to any other sources in this account. These two facts are important as they give us insight into our lost book and into the main source for our lost book.

We must ask why Ptolemy might choose snakes over crows as the divine escort. There are several possible reasons. Though it's unlikely, there actually could have been snakes that led them to the temple. Ptolemy was likely on the journey to the oracle of Ammon, but we don't know if Aristobulus was there. Perhaps both heard that animals led Alexander's group to the temple, and Aristobulus's source said crows while Ptolemy's said snakes. If it was open to interpretation, or if Ptolemy simply chose to disregard the truth, snakes would have been an understandable choice as divine guidance, especially if those snakes were cobras. There's no indication that Ptolemy gave the species, but just that he said snakes. Regardless, snakes were sacred animals to the Egyptians, and specifically cobras, which were considered guardians to Egyptian kingship and could be found often on the royal headdress of the pharaoh. Could Ptolemy, writing his *History* while he was considering proclaiming himself, or after he had proclaimed himself, king of Egypt, be inserting these snakes as divine appointment of Alexander as king of Egypt and thereby claiming that through Alexander, he, Ptolemy, was the rightful king? It seems quite possible.

However they were led, they came through the desert and finally to the Temple of Ammon, which rested in an oasis. Arrian recounts that this oasis featured a spring that had the unbelievably helpful property of being cold during the hottest hours of the day and warm during the cold nights of the desert. This account seems not to have come from Ptolemy but more likely from Herodotus's *Histories,* where the father of history states:

> The Ammonians have another spring besides that which rises from the salt. The water of this stream is lukewarm at early dawn; at the time when the market fills up it is much cooler; by noon it has grown quite cold; at this time, therefore, they water their gardens. As afternoon advances the coldness goes off, till, about sunset, the water is once more lukewarm; still the heat increases, and at midnight it boils. After this time it again begins to cool, and grows less and less hot till morning comes. This spring is called "The Fountain of the Sun."

In an editor's note in a copy of Arrian's *Anabasis* from 1893, it is claimed that modern travelers have verified the existence of this spring. Besides the spring, this oasis was said to produce salt of a very fine quality.

Because of all this, Arrian tells us, "Alexander then was struck with wonder at the place, and consulted the oracle of the god. Having heard what was agreeable to his wishes, as he himself said, he set out on the journey back to Egypt." Diodorus gives a more detailed account of Alexander's consulting the oracle, and so we must assume this does not come from our lost book. He states that Alexander is told to consider himself the son of the god he is addressing, that he will rule the whole earth, and that all of Philip's murderers have been punished. Then, finally, there is another disagreement between Aristobulus and Ptolemy; the former says Alexander took the same route back that he had taken to the oasis, while the latter says he took a more direct route back to Memphis. This would seem to be of little importance, but one must ask: why do Aristobulus and Ptolemy disagree on the crows and snakes and on the route back to Memphis? If both writers went on the journey, it would seem they would relate at least the route to Memphis as the same. If one of them went and the other is relying on an incorrect source, that would explain the discrepancies. Or neither of them might have gone on the journey and were relying on the words of oth-

Map 3. Alexander's route from Egypt to India.

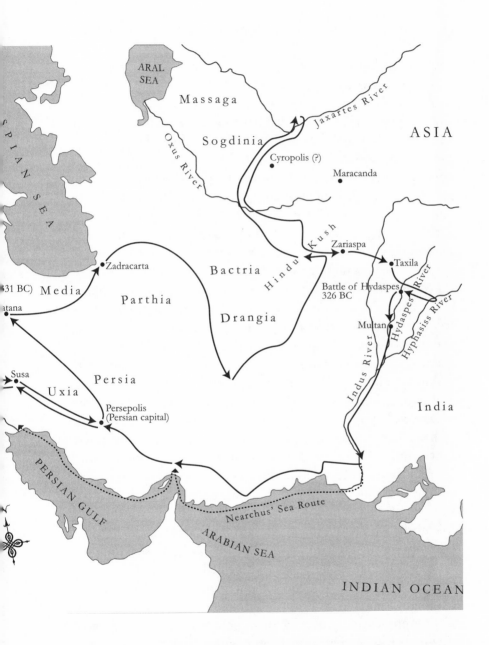

ers, and one of them is off—if we assume one of the accounts is correct.

So is our lost book the more accurate or not? Of course, it is impossible to say, but consider this: there is a strong likelihood that Ptolemy went on the journey to the oracle of Ammon. There is less of a likelihood that Aristobulus went, if he was truly an engineer as later scholars claim. Ptolemy might have had reason to turn crows into snakes, as one is more sacred to the Egyptians than the other. However, he probably wasn't writing his *History* for the benefit of an Egyptian audience, but a Greek one. Does that mean that snakes truly led Alexander and his entourage to the oasis? It does not, but they might have seen snakes and taken that for a sign. Regardless, the sources seem to agree on the general story, that Alexander went to the oasis, consulted the oracle, heard good news, and returned to Memphis.

At Memphis, Alexander was met by emissaries and newly recruited soldiers sent by Antipater and cavalry from Thrace. He placed garrisons in Egypt and placed an Egyptian, Doloaspis, as governor. He held another procession of the army and more gymnastic and musical competitions. He reorganized his army, replacing officers who had died and separating a part of his army to leave in Egypt under the command of Peucestas, who was one of his shield bearers, and Balacrus. He placed Apollonius over Libya and Cleomenes over part of Arabia. Arrian remarks, "Alexander was said to have divided the government of Egypt among so many men, because he was surprised at the natural strength of the country, and he thought it unsafe to entrust the rule of the whole to a single person." This, most assuredly, does not come from Ptolemy, since Ptolemy, as he was writing his *History,* was that single person who ruled over all of Egypt. In fact, Arrian's comment seems somehow unfitting since ultimately the governorship of Egypt fell to one man (there were originally supposed to be two Egyptian governors, but one of them declined, leaving Doloaspis), and while there were two garrisons, they were in two different cities.

This was a method that Alexander had adopted in Anatolia, where he left a governor or satrap over the region and garrisons in the cities. The one distinction Egypt seems to have is that Alexander left an entire army there besides. There is no indication on what the size of this army was, but obviously Alexander saw the need to place an extra guard in Egypt, perhaps fearing an attack from Persian forces or even an insurrection by the local population, despite his assurance that he was the son of Zeus-Ammon and rightful ruler of Egypt.

It was now spring 331 BC. Alexander returned to Tyre, sacrificed, and held more competitions. His fleet was awaiting him there, and he ordered it to go to Peloponnesus to stop any resistance from the Spartans and their allies in Greece. Envoys from Athens also met him in Tyre and pleaded for the release of Athenians captured at Granicus. After this, Alexander set out for the Euphrates River. At this time he appointed Harpalus, son of Machatas, to oversee his treasury while on the march. Harpalus was one of Alexander's friends whom Philip had sent into exile, along with Ptolemy. In detailing the story of Harpalus—that he was returned from exile and made treasurer by Alexander, then deserted, then was convinced to return without any punishment from Alexander—Arrian tells us that when his friends returned from exile, Alexander appointed all of them to important positions, notably Ptolemy to bodyguard, although this actually happened years after his return from exile. He was surely one of the Companions, however, and this supports the idea that Ptolemy was almost always near Alexander, rode with him in every battle, and was close at hand during their long journeys into and beyond the Persian Empire.

In July or August 331 BC, Alexander crossed the Euphrates, which he found unguarded because those set to defend it had retreated upon hearing that Alexander's whole army approached. Alexander marched on through Mesopotamia. It was assumed that Darius had gathered an army and was waiting for Alexander somewhere in the area. This proved correct when some of

Darius's scouts were captured. These scouts reported that Darius had an even larger army than he had had at Issus and that he was camped by the Tigris River, waiting to stop Alexander from crossing. But when Alexander reached the Tigris, he found no army and crossed the fast-moving waters without opposition.

Alexander marched on. Arrian, probably drawing from our lost book, tells us, "Alexander moved on through the country of Assyria, with the Gordyenian Mountains on his left and the Tigris on his right. On the fourth day out from where he crossed the river his scouts brought him reports that some enemy cavalry could be seen in the plain, but they could not estimate their numbers." It turned out to only be about a thousand cavalry, and Alexander took a contingent of his own cavalry and pursued them. Some escaped, some were killed, but from the few that were taken prisoner it was learned that Darius was not far off and had with him a large army.

eight

THE END OF THE PERSIAN EMPIRE

D ARIUS'S ARMY, IN WHAT WOULD BE CALLED THE BATTLE OF Gaugamela, was massive. Modern estimates put it at around eighty thousand to one hundred thousand soldiers. Plutarch says Darius fielded a million men. Arrian says a million infantry and forty thousand cavalry, plus fifteen war elephants (this is the first time elephants were reported as being used in warfare). Curtius Rufus gives the number at forty-five thousand cavalry and two hundred thousand infantry. The true number is unknown, but suffice it to say that this was an army of a scale that rivaled or surpassed Darius's force at Issus. We know that many of the numbers from Arrian come from Ptolemy's *History,* yet we don't know where Ptolemy got his numbers. Were they from the official account by Callisthenes? If that were the case, then the numbers would surely be inaccurate, as Callisthenes was paid to write clear propaganda in favor of Alexander. This official historian would have increased the numbers of the Persian army to make a victory by Alexander that much more profound. However, Ptolemy might be giving the numbers that the scouts gave Alexander, since he could have been there to hear it himself. Here we must wonder whether Ptolemy kept a diary or journal while on campaign or if he relied on his memory of almost forty years. Of course, we'll probably never know.

Alexander's army is generally given as forty-seven thousand total, with seven thousand cavalry and forty thousand infantry. Darius's obvious numerical advantage was offset by a few factors. As has been mentioned, the Macedonians were equipped with longer spears and heavier armor. They had the benefit of being, for the most part, highly trained, seasoned warriors. They were battle hardened and under the command of a successful, charismatic leader. In addition, reports indicated that Darius feared a night attack, so when the battle was imminent, he had his troops stay awake during the night. Alexander's army was well rested. Also, Alexander had a plan.

According to Arrian, and here we must wonder if this is directly from our lost book, Parmenion suggested a night attack to Alexander. Here again, Alexander informed his second-in-command that this was the wrong strategy. Alexander wanted his victory to be without blemish; he didn't wish Darius to be able to say that the Macedonians won by treachery. Also, he deemed it too perilous a proposition because night attacks were hard to control. Finally, such an attack would be an admission that Alexander's army was inferior, and Alexander could not agree to that.

By the time the armies found each other and were prepared for battle, it was autumn 331 BC. Darius had chosen a wide-open space, learning from his mistake at Issus. He ordered the ground to be leveled, the better to move his chariots. Darius had encamped his army at Arbela. This is sometimes given as the location of the battle, but modern scholars say it was at a spot known as Gaugamela.

Aristobulus says that a document detailing Darius's plan of battle was captured afterward, and perhaps Ptolemy himself was able to see this document. In any case, this is how Arrian says Darius's army was positioned:

> His left wing was held by the Bactrian cavalry together with the Dahae and Arachosians; next to them were Persian contingents, mixed cavalry and infantry; the Susians next to the Persians, and the Cadusians next to the Susians. . . . Placed on the right wing were the troops from Hollow Syria and Mesopotamia, and further to the right the Medes; then in sequence the Parthyaeans . . . Sacae . . . Topeirians . . . Hyrcanians . . . Albanians . . . Sacesinians, all these filling the line up to the center of the entire phalanx. In the center with King Darius were stationed the King's Kinsmen, the Persian palace guard . . . Indians . . . transplanted Carians . . . and the Mardian archers. The Uxians, Babylonians, Red Sea people, and Sittacenians were drawn up behind in depth. In advance of the left wing, facing Alexander's right, were posted the Scythian cavalry, about a thousand Bactrians, and a hundred scythe-chariots. The elephants were positioned, together with fifty chariots, in front of Darius's royal squadron. In advance of the right wing were posted Armenian and Cappadocian cavalry with fifty scythe-chariots. The Greek mercenaries were drawn up on both sides of Darius and his attendant Persians directly opposite the Macedonian phalanx, as the only troops capable of matching it.

Alexander's army was arrayed not in a straight line, as Darius's was, but with each wing at a forty-five-degree angle away from the Persian army, with the troops in what is called an échelon formation. This allowed Alexander's army to be in position to meet the flanking maneuvers that would obviously come from Darius. Alexander's right wing was held by the Companion cavalry and several other squadrons of cavalry; next to them were Macedonian infantry, then additional infantry. On the left were the Thessalian cavalry, Thracians, the Odrysian cavalry, and additional cavalry, all under the command of Parmenion. Archers and Agrianians were placed in back with additional infantry.

As the two armies came together, Alexander began to move his right wing farther and farther right, stretching out his line to its limits. Darius countered by stretching his line farther and farther left to meet Alexander. Ptolemy would have been close to Alexander in battle and might have even known the king's plans. Regardless, he would have been exhilarated, racing into battle, watching the numerous enemies advancing while he charged forward to meet them. It would have been a rush, but also probably terrifying. Who knew if Alexander's strategy to create a gap in the Persian line would work? Even if it resulted in a short victory, would they be able to break this massive army? Darius had learned since Issus; the scouts said he had more men. Alexander couldn't go on winning forever.

Alexander ordered some of the mercenary cavalry to charge at the Persians' extended left wing. This charge was beaten back with superior numbers. They tried again with assistance from the light cavalry but were not able to break the line. Alexander's men suffered heavy losses in this engagement but were finally able to push the Persian forces out of rank. At the same time, Darius sent his scythe-chariots toward Alexander and his Companion cavalry. The chariots proved unequal to the task. The Agrianians and javelin throwers, who were stationed in front of the Companions, threatened the chariot horses with javelins and grabbed the reins to stop the chariots and kill the riders. Other chariots they let pass through their ranks by parting; thus the chariots injured no one but were captured by the troops and grooms in the rear of the army, near the camp.

Alexander ordered an attack farther to the right, and the Persian army stretched farther to its left. It stretched so far that a gap appeared in its lines, and as soon as Alexander saw that the gap had formed, he ordered those around him into a wedge formation and they broke through the gap, heading directly for Darius. At this point, our lost book tells us that Darius saw this direct assault, turned, and fled. According to Diodorus and Curtius Rufus, there was a brief spear battle between Alexander and Darius in which Darius's charioteer was killed. The Persian army thought it was Darius and despaired. It is telling that our lost book doesn't mention this, as Ptolemy would have been near Alexander during the fighting and would probably have had the best chance to observe any spear throwing between Alexander and Darius.

At the same time, the Persian left wing broke and began to retreat. The Macedonians pursued them and killed as many as they could. Yet some of the Persian cavalry and Indian cavalry broke through and made it to the Macedonian baggage, where they began to kill the men guarding the baggage and incite the prisoners to attack their guards. Seeing this, commanders from the rear phalanx attacked the Persians from the rear and put a stop to their assault.

Alexander's left wing was not so quickly victorious. Arrian tells us that Parmenion sent a messenger to Alexander asking for aid. This caused Alexander to halt his immediate pursuit of Darius and turn his cavalry back to attack the Persian right wing from behind. Here Parmenion is cast as a liability: unable to hold his line, he is forced to call on his king for help. This would appear to be part of the propaganda against Parmenion, so we should take this report with more than a grain of salt. To ask for reinforcements in the midst of a pitched battle is not, in itself, any crime or condemnation of a commander. Alexander could have denied Parmenion's request, or he could have sent some troops to help his second-in-command while continuing his pursuit of Darius. All we can say with any degree of certainty is that Alexander broke off his pursuit of Darius at first and came to the aid of Parmenion. All of our sources agree on that account.

In the fierce fighting that ensued, Alexander's friend Hephaestion was injured, and sixty of the Companions were killed. The Persian right wing then broke, and every man attempted to escape as quickly as possible. Alexander regained control of those he could and set off again in pursuit of Darius.

Parmenion went and captured the baggage the Persians had brought with them to the battle, along with some elephants and camels. Ptolemy probably joined Alexander on his race to find Darius, so his *History* would probably be our and Arrian's best source. Thus, when Arrian describes the pursuit of Darius, we can confidently say this comes from our lost book.

Alexander and his Companions crossed the river Lycus, which is also called Zabatus and is a tributary of the Tigris. Here he made camp and let the riders and horses rest for a little while. Their minds might have been set on capturing the Persian king, but they had just had a hard day of fighting and riding, and they needed their rest. A meal was probably taken, water resupplied from the river. There would have been discussion of the battle, the glorious defeat of the much-larger Persian army, and speculation about the path Darius would have taken and what his next plans might be. At midnight, Alexander resumed his pursuit and headed toward Arbela, where the Persians had camped before the Battle of Gaugamela. Darius had not stopped at Arbela, or at least not for long, because Alexander did not find him there. Yet Alexander did take the camp and was able to capture plenty of treasure, including Darius's chariot, bow, and shield, just as he had after Issus.

During the pursuit, Alexander would have received word of the outcome of the battle. Arrian, once again probably getting his figures from Ptolemy, tells us three hundred thousand enemy were killed and many more taken prisoner. As usual, Ptolemy seems to inflate the numbers to unbelievable proportions. If the Persian army was the more reasonable, yet high, eighty thousand to one hundred thousand, then it is possible that a third were killed and the rest taken prisoner. In Arrian's account, there is some confusion on the number of casualties suffered by Alexander. He says one hundred of Alexander's men were killed and one thousand of his horses "were lost either from wounds or from fatigue in the pursuit, nearly half of them belonging to the Companion cavalry." This makes one think that perhaps the one

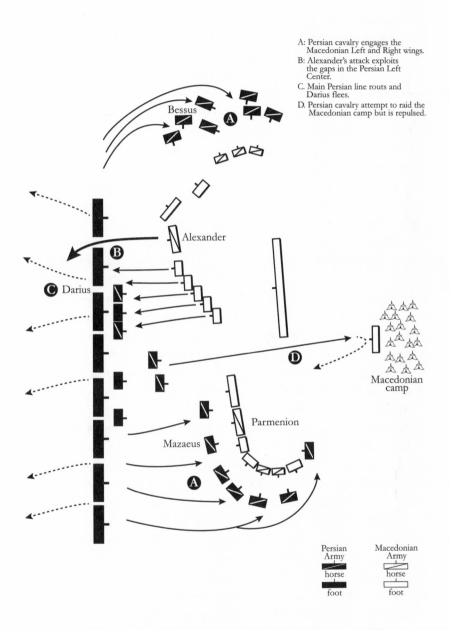

A: Persian cavalry engages the
   Macedonian Left and Right wings.
B: Alexander's attack exploits
   the gaps in the Persian Left
   Center.
C. Main Persian line routs and
   Darius flees.
D. Persian cavalry attempt to raid the
   Macedonian camp but is repulsed.

Bessus

Ⓐ

Alexander

Ⓑ

Ⓒ Darius

Macedonian
camp

Ⓓ

Parmenion

Mazaeus

Ⓐ

Persian
Army
horse
foot

Macedonian
Army
horse
foot

Map 4. The Battle of Gaugamela, 331 B.C.

hundred men killed died in the pursuit, and so Arrian doesn't give a figure for Alexander's total casualties. It is hard to believe that Ptolemy didn't give a reckoning in his *History*, so we must consider the possibility that Arrian didn't feel the need to give such details. It is hard to say. Other sources give the incredible number of total Macedonian casualties as three hundred men slain.

Regardless of the specific numbers, this was the end of the Battle of Gaugamela and thus the end of the Persian Empire. Darius continued his flight, and at some point Alexander felt the pursuit was lost and so called it off. Darius was accompanied by the Bactrian cavalry and also by the Persians called the King's Kinsmen, and some of the Apple-Bearers, who are sometimes called the Immortals, a group of elite imperial guards comparable to Alexander's Companions. He traveled through the mountains to the north and into Media. Media was the homeland of the Medes, an ancient people who had once controlled a great kingdom of their own but had been enveloped into the Persian Empire in 550 BC. Here again it would seem someone learned of Darius's movement after the fact, but no one mentions a source for this information.

It is said that Darius traveled into Media because he believed Alexander would go to Babylon and Susa, the gems of the empire, after the battle. If this were true, then Darius, at least once, was able to predict Alexander's movement, for he did go first to Babylon, where leaders and citizens of the city met him with gifts and welcomed him as their new king. Alexander had been prepared to fight for Babylon, so it must have been a great relief that he would not need to besiege the great city-state. Entering Babylon, with Ptolemy at his side, Alexander must have felt fortune's favor, to be welcomed into this city of the fabled hanging gardens as a great king after he had just won such a resounding victory over the Persian army. Could he have looked to the heavens and seen his father, not Philip, but Zeus-Ammon, king of the gods?

Alexander ordered the Babylonians to rebuild all the temples that had been destroyed by the Persian king Xerxes, especially those temples for Belus. This was a much-revered Babylonian god who was often associated with Zeus, though he was at other times called a god of war. Strabo calls the great ziggurat in Babylon the Tomb of Belus, and it is indicated by some that Belus was a founding king of Babylon. Alexander then offered sacrifice to Belus and performed other religious rites particular to the Babylonians. Arrian says little else about Alexander's stay in Babylon.

Curtius Rufus goes into much more detail. He states that Alexander's army stayed in the city thirty-four days and did nothing except revel, drink, and debauch themselves. He does not give any sources for his information but says plainly that women, married or not, of any age, were all prostitutes and that the city was, as a whole, immoral and what later writers might call a den of sin. This information would almost surely be lacking from Ptolemy's *History*, partly because any hint at unseemly behavior by Alexander and his Companions would probably not jibe with the thesis of Ptolemy's work, but also because part of it must be complete exaggeration.

After this, Alexander marched toward Susa, another great city. It is said that the city was surrendered to Alexander without a fight, and the treasury of fifty thousand talents was handed over to him. A Greek talent weighed roughly 57 pounds. If these talents were all of gold, then a single talent would be worth over a million dollars today. Of course, these conversions are far from perfect. Needless to say, Alexander had now gained unimaginable wealth.

Here Alexander also found many Greek statues that Xerxes had plundered on his conquest so many generations before. These Alexander had returned to the Athenians. At Susa, Alexander performed religious sacrifices and held a torch race and gymnastic contests. He sent money back to Antipater in Macedon to help in the struggle against the Spartans. Alexander rearranged his army, separating infantry regiments according to nationality and establishing two companies in each squadron of cavalry. From here, Alexander marched on to Persia.

First he came to the land of the Uxians, a tribe that lived in the region between Susa and the Persian capital of Persepolis. Here our lost book tells us that the Uxians who were subjects of the Persians surrendered to Alexander. But some of the tribe, who lived in the mountains, were not subjects of the Persians and sent word to Alexander that they would not allow him to march through their pass unless he paid the same toll that the Persians were required to pay. Alexander sent messengers back to say that he would pay the toll if the Uxians would come to the defiles, steep-sided narrow gorges, that were along the main path through the mountains.

Alexander then took a select detachment of troops, and, with the help of Susian guides, they went off along a different road from that of the main army. The Companions were with those who went with Alexander, so Ptolemy would have been with his king during this night march into the Uxian defiles. First Alexander fell on the villages of the Uxians and killed many while they were still sleeping. It is said he gained much booty, but it is hard to imagine what wealth the Uxians would have had compared to Babylon and Susa. Then Alexander split his force, which was roughly fifteen thousand men. Part of his force went with Craterus to a spot that Alexander believed the Uxians would fall back to if they were forced from the defiles. Then he took his remaining troops and force-marched to the defiles. They reached the defiles before the Uxians and so were able to command higher ground and array themselves in battle formation. The Uxians took flight without coming into conflict with Alexander's men. Alexander chased them down, and many were killed in the pursuit, while many died from falling off the defiles into the rocky gorges below. The rest fled just to the spot where Alexander had believed they would go and were destroyed by Craterus.

Our lost book makes a point to say that Darius's mother entreated Alexander on behalf of the Uxians to "grant them the privilege of inhabiting the land." That is, she begged that the Uxians who survived should be allowed to continue to live in their homeland and not be slaughtered or sold into slavery. Alexander relented and allowed them to stay; in exchange he commanded them to pay a tribute of one hundred horses, five hundred oxen, and thirty thousand sheep. The fact that Ptolemy recorded that it was Darius's mother who asked for this on behalf of the Uxians is telling. It allows Alexander to grant the Uxians their land because of his affection for Darius's mother. This fact, if it is a fact, doesn't seem to carry the propaganda that accentuates much of Ptolemy's work. Arrian, it would seem, includes it because it is not mentioned in his other sources. This gives this detail the air of authenticity because Ptolemy would have been present to hear such a request from Darius's mother. However, there does seem to be a desire on Ptolemy's part to show Alexander as compassionate, at least occasionally. Perhaps it was known that Alexander allowed the surviving Uxians to live in their homeland, and Ptolemy was giving his readers a reason for Alexander's actions: his respect for this noble woman.

Next Alexander split his forces again, sending Parmenion with the baggage and heavily armored troops along the carriage road and taking with himself the Companion cavalry, the Macedonian infantry, the light cavalry, the Agrianians, and the archers, and engaged a forced march through the mountains to the Persian Gates. Like many other "gates" in ancient times, this was the name for a pass, now known as Tang-e Meyran. When Alexander reached the pass, he found Ariobarzanes, the viceroy of Persis, the region where Persepolis lay, with forty thousand infantry and seven hundred cavalry camped near the gate. They had also built a wall across the pass in order to further impede Alexander's progress.

Alexander tried at first to take the wall but was repelled in this attempt. Much as he did in the Uxian defiles, Alexander learned, this time from prisoners, of another route by which he could take the Persians unawares. He left some of his army by the wall so it could attack when the moment was right. With him he took the shield-bearing guards, Perdiccas's brigade, the lightest-armed archers, the Agrianians, the royal squadron of Companion cavalry, and another regiment of cavalry and marched by night through the mountainous route. He met the first guard at first light and destroyed them. He met the second guard and was able to kill most of them, but the third guard was able to escape. Yet instead of fleeing to Ariobarzanes, which was the concern, they fled into the mountains simply to escape Alexander's wrath. So he was able to attack the enemy's camp without being detected. When he fell on them, Craterus attacked the fortifications and quickly took them, as the Persians were now being attacked from many sides at once.

Here our lost book tells us that the Persians fleeing Craterus on one side and Alexander on the other fell into a trap that Alexander had laid near the wall in the pass. He stationed Ptolemy there with three thousand infantry. Ptolemy ordered his men to attack when the Persians came in close and quickly cut them to pieces. This account places Ptolemy, the author, in the center of the action and gives him a starring role in this engagement. We must consider the possibility that Ptolemy has exaggerated his role. Curtius Rufus seems to indicate that Alexander split up his forces between Craterus, Philotas, Polyperchon, Amyntas, and Coenus and doesn't mention Ptolemy at all.

If Arrian had stated that Ptolemy alone had claimed his role in this battle, then we might be safe in assuming Ptolemy exaggerated. But Arrian doesn't make this claim, so there is a chance that both Aristobulus and Ptolemy agree on this account. That would add weight to the possibility that Ptolemy did lead those three thousand infantry. Ptolemy was surely part of this battle, and so we must consider that this is the first moment that he makes an appearance in his own narrative. It is still possible that Ptolemy wrote a strict memoir, but based on the selections

Arrian uses, this seems implausible, mainly because one would think that Ptolemy would have shown up in Arrian's book as a major character sooner than the battle at the Persian Gates. Instead, it seems likely that it was autobiography mixed with straightforward history.

Regardless, Alexander had taken the Persian Gates, though Ariobarzanes was able to escape. Alexander then marched quickly to Persepolis, the Persian capital. Several of the ancient sources mention that along the way, Alexander's army met with a score of Greeks who had been mutilated by the cutting off of limbs, noses, and other body parts. Alexander offered to send these Greeks home, but they decided to stay in Persia, and Alexander gave them money, clothing, and cattle. Arrian does not mention this episode, so we must conclude that Ptolemy's *History* doesn't mention it either.

At Persepolis, Alexander captured the royal treasury, which Diodorus and Curtius say amounted to one hundred twenty thousand talents. Arrian doesn't mention this. Finally, Alexander burned down the palace in Persepolis, against Parmenion's wishes, as a planned act of vengeance against the Persians for what they had done to the Greeks. Most of the ancient sources—Diodorus, Plutarch, and Curtius Rufus—state that the palace was handed over to soldiers to plunder but that the burning of the palace came about in a drunken revelry and was instigated by a specific courtesan, Thais.

Thais is an interesting character in her own right, and it would be wonderful to have a complete and detailed history of this intriguing woman. Unfortunately, we are only left with tantalizing scraps of information. She was a *hetera*, or a courtesan, a woman of sophistication and education who was a companion to her patron. Most *hetera* were also the lovers of their patrons, though they should not be seen strictly as prostitutes. Thais may have been attached to Alexander at some point, but eventually she became Ptolemy's lover and would go on to marry him and bear him three children. But she was never his queen after he became king of Egypt, and their children were never considered his heirs.

So if the tale of Alexander and his men drunkenly setting fire to the Persian palace at the instigation of Thais is true, Ptolemy would have good reasons to not set that down in his book. It would stain the reputation of Alexander and his men, Ptolemy included, and it would place the blame on Thais, who would be Ptolemy's wife. While Ptolemy might attempt to be accurate in his narrative, it would be in his best interests to gloss over this part of the story. So instead, he claims Alexander burned the palace as part of a plan to seek revenge for the supposed crimes of the Persians.

nine

IN PURSUIT OF DARIUS

Alexander now turned his mind toward capturing Darius. He knew the Persian king to be in Media, so that is where he marched. Alexander was told that Darius was forming another army and that he intended to meet him in battle once again. But when he finally arrived in Media with his army in battle formation, he learned that Darius's army was not prepared to fight and that it seemed the Persian king would flee yet again. Alexander then learned that Darius was about five days ahead of him. At this point, on the verge of capturing the enemy he had sought so long, Alexander paid the Greek allies their wages and told them that if they wished to enlist they could do so of their own free will or else they could leave at that moment. This seems to have been a calculated move on Alexander's part. While in hot pursuit of Darius, he offered at least some of his soldiers the chance to go home. Whether it was a ploy or not, it seems to have worked, for many of the men reenlisted. This gave Alexander the motivated, battle-tested troops he needed to continue this campaign.

He then ordered Parmenion to take a large body of troops and march into Hyrcania, a land at the south end of the Caspian

Sea in what is today Iran and Turkmenistan. He ordered Cleitus, the leader of the royal squadron, who had been left behind in Susa because of illness, to head straight for Parthia, as this was where Alexander intended to go. Parthia lies near Hyrcania, in northeast Iran. Alexander took several squads of cavalry, the Macedonian phalanx, the Agrianians, and the archers and set out once more to capture Darius. He pressed forward at a relentless pace, leaving behind any exhausted soldiers and horses that died from the exertion. They came upon the Caspian Gates, a defile at the southeastern corner of the Caspian Sea. Many of Darius's companions had abandoned their king and were captured by Alexander along the way. Many simply left Darius and went into the mountains, presumably making their way back home, having given up hope of any Persian victory.

Alexander then stopped and let his men rest awhile. He hoped to gain provisions from the nearby land so he could continue his pursuit across what he was told was desert. At this point, Alexander received word that Darius had been arrested by his companions: Nabarzanes, a cavalry commander; Bessus, the viceroy of Bactria; and Barsaentes of the Arachotians and Drangians. Bessus had assumed command of the party that held Darius. Alexander immediately set out after them, taking the Companion cavalry, the light cavalry, and selected foot soldiers, who were given mounts to ride. Alexander pursued relentlessly through day and night, only allowing his party short breaks to rest. Alexander learned that Bessus planned to give Darius to Alexander in the hopes that there might be some quarter given for this action.

It is hard to say exactly what happened next to Darius. Our lost book would appear to be silent on whether Bessus and the other captors changed their minds or if there was some calamity that led to lethal results. In any event, while Alexander was in pursuit, having taken a quicker route in the hopes of catching up with Darius and his captors, Darius was killed. Arrian states that Nabarzanes and Barsaentes, the commander and the viceroy, slew the Persian king. One must wonder at the reasoning behind this death. If the captors truly had decided to surrender Darius to Alexander, then killing him made no sense. But perhaps they hadn't come to such a final conclusion and what Alexander heard was simply one of several options the captors were considering. The most logical answer is that they feared Alexander and, knowing that he wanted Darius, thought that by killing him and abandoning his body they could escape and Alexander would not follow. Curtius Rufus gives a detailed account of Darius's last days, but since his source is not Ptolemy, we'll simply let it be said that Darius was killed by his captors and his body left behind in their flight.

Alexander had Darius's body sent back to Persepolis, to be buried in the royal tomb with all honors. Thus, Darius III, king of Persia, was laid to rest in July 330 BC. If Darius's captors thought that killing him and fleeing would stop Alexander's pursuit, they were at least partly right. Although Alexander once more formed his army together, he did not continue his heated pursuit but marched into Hyrcania. He resolved to go after the Greek mercenaries who had been with Darius in his flight but had left the king and gone into the mountains of Hyrcania.

Alexander divided his army into three parts. He led the most and lightest-armored men through the most difficult path through the mountains. Craterus, with his own brigade and that of Amyntas, was sent against a local tribe called the Tapurians, and Erigyius took possession of the remaining troops and the baggage and went by the main road. Alexander advanced and left guards at intervals in case they were being followed, since he didn't know exactly where the Greek mercenaries were.

Alexander's contingent passed through the mountains and came to a small river in a plain. Here Nabarzanes, the cavalry commander and one of the supposed murderers of Darius, along with Phrataphernes, a viceroy, and other distinguished Persians came and surrendered to Alexander. Alexander accepted their surrender. Next he traveled deeper into Hyrcania, arriving at the capital of the region, Zadracarta. Here he reconvened with the rest of his army. Craterus had not managed to find the Greek mercenaries but had gained the capitulation of the local tribes and villages. Erigyius arrived with the baggage and wagons without having run into any considerable trouble. At Zadracarta, Alexander was met by Autophradates, the viceroy of Tapuria, who surrendered. Also surrendering was Artabazus—a Persian nobleman who had been exiled in Macedon for ten years and had met a young Alexander before returning to Persia to be part of Darius's court—and Artabazus's sons. Alexander restored Autophradates to his vice regal position and kept Artabazus and his sons in an honored position in his army, as he believed them to be honorable for their great loyalty to Darius.

Next came envoys from the Greek mercenaries, who were nearby. The envoys asked Alexander to make peace with them and let them go free. Alexander replied that he would make no deal with them and that they should present themselves to him and he would decide their fate. As we have seen, Alexander held a particular grudge against Greek mercenaries who fought on the side of the Persians. Their crime was betrayal, something Alexander could not easily forgive. As Arrian puts it, drawing from Aristobulus and/or Ptolemy, "He commanded them to come in a body and surrender, leaving it to him to treat them as he pleased or to preserve themselves as best they could." The envoys said they surrendered themselves and their comrades to Alexander and asked that he send someone from his forces to retrieve the remaining mercenaries and assure that they made it safely to Alexander. He sent Andronicus, son of Agerrhus, and Artabazus. Thus one of Darius's noblemen was sent to retrieve Darius's Greek mercenaries and lead them to their fate.

In the meantime, Alexander marched against a people known as the Mardians, who probably lived west of Hyrcania, near the Caspian Gates. Arrian, here probably drawing from our lost book, tells us that the Mardians did not expect Alexander to enter their land because it was very mountainous and the people were very poor. Yet Alexander did attack. He hunted them down, killed many, and took many prisoners. They fled into the mountains, and he pursued them there until they were forced to surrender. He placed Autophradates, the newly appointed viceroy over the Tapurians, as viceroy over the Mardians as well. I think the story of Alexander's conquest of the Mardians provides an insight into his motivations, and possibly Ptolemy intended it to be so. He conquered the Mardians not because they were a threat or were wealthy, but simply because they were there and posed a potential threat to instability in his empire. In order for Alexander to conquer the world, he needed to conquer every region he came across, if possible. This is the portrait that the lost book hopes to paint. Even when Alexander most likely didn't conquer all of Arabia, Ptolemy's *History* indicates that he captured much of it. Yet there is nothing negative in this portrait. Ptolemy, and one assume his audience as well, would have seen Alexander's pursuit of dominion as a glorious task.

On returning to his camp, Alexander found that Darius's Greek mercenaries had been delivered to him; along with them were some Greek envoys who had been sent to Darius. He released most of the envoys except those of the Spartans, whom he kept as prisoners under guard. The mercenaries he split into two groups: those who had joined Darius before the Macedonians had forced an alliance with the Greeks and those who had joined Darius afterward. Those who had joined before, he let go free. Those who had joined after, he conscripted to his own army, but he told them he would pay them the same salary as Darius had paid them. He put them under the command of Andronicus, who, with Artabazus, had led the mercenaries to Alexander in the first place.

Alexander now marched back to Zadracarta, where he sacrificed and held contests for fifteen days. From here he marched east through Parthia and into the region of Areia, to a city called Susia. Here the viceroy of the Areians, Satibarzanes, came out to meet Alexander as a friend. Alexander accepted him and allowed him to continue in his vice regal position. He assigned one of the Companions, Anaxippus, and forty of the new horse javelin men to act as guards to protect the Areians while Alexander's army marched through. It was at this time, our lost book would tell us, that Alexander received word that Bessus was amassing an army, had declared himself the new Persian king, and had adopted the name Artaxerxes.

Bessus's move was not unusual. It was common practice for Persian kings, and really any kings of this period, to be assassinated and for those who ordered the murder to then take the throne. Bessus had some relation to Darius, and the satrap of Bactria was considered by some to be next in line to the throne. The problem for Bessus, and the reason most historians don't refer to him as a Persian king with the name Artaxerxes, was that when he came to the throne, his kingdom was all but gone. The Persian Empire, for the most part, belonged to Alexander, making him the new Persian king. Alexander had now conquered Greece, Anatolia, Syria, and Egypt, parts of Arabia, Mesopotamia, and Persia, not to mention several other regions. What lay before him was Bactria and a pretender to the Persian throne.

Reports indicated that Bessus had some loyal Persians with him, as well as many Bactrians, and that he was expecting the Scythians to join him soon. So Alexander took his army and marched toward Bactria. He did not get very far before he learned that Satibarzanes, the viceroy, had betrayed him and killed the Companion Anaxippus and the forty horse javelin men. The viceroy had gathered and armed the Areians with a plan to go to the aid of Bessus and help put a stop to Alexander. Once again, Alexander's intelligence was sound, and he acted decisively. He halted his march to Bactria and headed back to Artacoana, the capital city of the Areian region. Arrian often lists the military groups that went with Alexander on a particular mission or were under his command during a battle. Based on Arrian's assertions at the beginning of his work, these lists must have come from Ptolemy and/or Aristobulus. Since Aristobulus is, at one point, recognized as an engineer in Alexander's army, it seems unlikely that Arrian would get these lists solely from that source. So it is either Ptolemy alone who gives these details, or both Ptolemy and Aristobulus do and they agree, thus Arrian doesn't point out where they differ. Of course Ptolemy was not working solely from memory. There is good reason to believe he used sources of his own, most notably the *Royal Diary* of Alexander, which may have been the chronicle written by Callisthenes or the royal secretary Eumenes.

In any case, we must presume that our lost book tells us that Alexander broke off from his main army with the following troops: the Companion cavalry, some horse javelin men, the archers, the Agrianians, and the infantry regiments of Amyntas and Coenus. They traveled about seventy miles in two days, factoring in periods of rest; they must have kept a steady pace of two to three miles per hour wearing armor and carrying all their gear. Other ancient sources give greater speeds for forced marches, but this was a lightning quick response, and Satibarzanes was not ready for it. On hearing that Alexander was close to his city, he took a few horsemen and fled. The rest of the men Satibarzanes had gathered deserted him and attempted to flee back to their homes. Alexander had them quickly captured. Some were killed, the rest sold into slavery. This, it must be assumed, was because of Satibarzanes's betrayal in acting as a friend to Alexander and then revolting against him and killing one of the Companions. Just as Thebes had revolted against Alexander and suffered greatly, the Areians did as well.

Instead of heading north into Bactria, Alexander first turned south and entered the land of the Drangians (who are also called the Zarangaeans). Barsaentes, the other reported assassin of Darius, was in control of this region, but on hearing of Alexander's approach, he fled to the Indians. The Indians subsequently arrested him and sent him to Alexander. Given his crime of killing a king, he was executed by orders of Alexander.

One then wonders what became of the other supposed murderer of Darius, Nabarzanes, who had surrendered to Alexander
earlier. There is no account in Arrian of this man's fate, so we
must consider that our lost book is also silent on the matter. Was
he kept as a prisoner, his life spared because he voluntarily surrendered? Did Alexander know of his hand in the killing of
Darius, or was this fact learned later? Nabarzanes may have been
executed for his crimes, but the histories say nothing on the subject.

ten

PLOTS, TRIALS, AND MURDER

HERE IS A BRIEF ACCOUNT OF THE FATES OF TWO OF THOSE very close to Alexander. Ptolemy's *History* would tell us that back when Alexander was in Egypt, he heard of a plot to kill him that was connected to Philotas, son of Parmenion. At the time, Alexander didn't put any credence into the accusations, but here in the land of the Drangians, the accusations were brought forth again. According to our lost book, there was clear and damning evidence against Philotas, and Alexander was convinced. This would not have been anything like a modern-day court case. Ptolemy's account was "that Philotas was brought before the Macedonians, that Alexander vehemently accused him, and that he defended himself from the charges. [Ptolemy] says also that the divulgers of the plot came forward and convicted [Philotas] and his accomplices both by clear proofs and especially because Philotas himself confessed that he had heard of a certain conspiracy which was being formed against Alexander."

Philotas's knowing of a plot to kill Alexander and not telling the king was reason enough to sentence him to death for treason. Our lost book would be silent on whether Philotas was tortured. In the end, he lost his life, along with those deemed to be his accomplices. The danger now rested with Parmenion, Philotas's father and Alexander's second-in-command. Parmenion, who had constantly been the voice of caution and was consistently ignored and proven wrong by Alexander—or at least that is the way our lost book would portray him. Parmenion, who had fought with Alexander's father, Philip, and had come to be the reliable commander of the left wing, who had never broken when faced with the task of holding his line in the face of overwhelming Persian numbers—would he break now at the news of his son's execution? He had already lost a son to disease. How would be bear losing another son at the hands of his king? Would he turn on Alexander and command those soldiers under him and who were loyal to him to rise up against their king?

Alexander did not want to find out. After ordering Philotas's death, he sent assassins out on orders to kill Parmenion, who was in Media with a strong force, before he could become a threat to the king. There may also have been some suspicion that Parmenion was involved in the plot to kill Alexander. This is probably the most our lost book has to say on the subject: Philotas was a traitor, Parmenion shared in his treason, and for this they were both killed. Curtius Rufus gives a much more detailed account, but it is most likely not taken from Ptolemy's work. He says that during Philotas's trial, Alexander claimed that Parmenion was the mastermind behind the plot to kill him. In Rufus's account, Alexander is judge, but also a first-rate lawyer, arguing for Philotas's guilt supported by the fact that only a person involved in the plot would remain silent when told of the plot by others. In the same account, before Philotas is killed he is tortured, which resulted in a full confession of the crime.

Curtius Rufus says that Alexander then ordered one Polydamas to go to Media with letters for Parmenion, one from

Alexander and the other ostensibly from Philotas. He also gave him instructions for Cleander, a general in Media. The orders for Cleander seemed to have been that he should place guards on Parmenion who would be ordered to kill him when he read the letters from Alexander. Thus it was that Parmenion was walking in a grove, surrounded by these guards, when Polydamas came to him and was hailed as his friend. Polydamas gave him the letters. First he read the one from Alexander, which seemed to be about simple military matters. Then he got to the letter that was supposed to be from his son. It is not revealed what this letter said, for as soon as Parmenion scanned it, he was attacked and stabbed many times. He died there, in the grove. His head was sent back to Alexander.

One must wonder why our lost book seems to cover the deaths of Philotas and Parmenion so briefly. We must entertain the possibility that Ptolemy was not so brief in discussing the trial and executions but that, for some reason, Arrian greatly condensed this part of the narrative. Arrian's goal, as he stated it, was to tell an accurate history of Alexander's anabasis, which refers to a journey from a coastline into the interior of a country. So it might be that Arrian wanted to focus more on the journey, the campaigns, and not on something like a dispute within Alexander's army. Of course, this might seem incredible. Alexander had his second-in-command murdered for less-than-clear motives. A modern reader might be astonished that Arrian would glaze over such an important detail. This is one moment where we can't know if our lost book has more to say on the matter and Arrian simply ignored it, or Ptolemy himself only touches briefly on something that might seem to cast Alexander in a negative light. For while Philotas's guilt seems to chiefly be that he ignored a possible threat to Alexander, Parmenion was only guilty of being a father. In none of the ancient sources is any evidence given to support the idea that Parmenion was part of a plot to kill Alexander. However, Parmenion did pose a potential threat to Alexander. He commanded many troops and could have led them against Alexander's remaining forces. Also, he was a member of the old guard, those Macedonians who had fought with Philip and were less likely to go along with Alexander's attempts to fuse Greek and Persian cultures in his court. And, as will be seen, being a member of this old guard occasionally proved to be fatal.

At this time, one of Alexander's most trusted commanders, Amyntas, along with his brothers, Polemo, Attains, and Simmias, were also accused of being part of the plot to kill Alexander. This was partly supported by the fact that when Philotas was arrested, Polemo fled and went to the enemy, presumably Bessus. Amyntas and his other brothers stayed and defended themselves successfully and won their freedom. They asked leave to get their wayward brother, which they did and returned him to presumably face trial. Arrian tells us that Amyntas's freedom did not gain him much because "soon after, as he was besieging a certain village, he was shot with an arrow and died of the wound; so that he derived no other advantage from his acquittal except that of dying with an unsullied reputation."

It was around this time, legend holds, that the Amazons came to Alexander's army. The queen of these women thought Alexander was a fine specimen and so slept with him for fourteen days in the hopes of having a child with him. If it was a daughter, she would keep her; if it was a son, she would send him back to his father. Arrian states plainly that Ptolemy did not mention the Amazons in his lost book, and he goes on to say he does not believe these stories concerning Alexander's coming into contact with Amazons because he believed that race had long been dead by the time of Alexander's conquests. Also around this time, Alexander is said to have begun to dress in the Persian manner. Plutarch tells us "at first he wore this habit only when conversed with the barbarians, or within doors, among his intimate friends and companions, but afterwards he appeared in it abroad, when he rode out, and at public audiences, a sight which the Macedonians beheld with grief; but they so respected his other virtues and good qualities that they felt it reasonable in some things to gratify his fancies and his passion of glory." Ptolemy's account seems to be silent on this matter, which is not surprising because he wrote it when he was about to, or had become, king of Egypt and had taken on many Egyptian customs and dress.

After the trial of Philotas, the murder of Parmenion, and the trials of Amyntas and his brothers, Alexander returned to the tasks at hand. He split the Companion cavalry in two and put Hephaestion as commander over one half and Cleitus the Black as commander of the other half. He marched into the land of the Ariaspians, who were later called the Euergetae. Alexander was received well by these people and treated them with honor in kind. Here he offered sacrifice to Apollo. He also arrested one of his bodyguards, Demetrius, for being implicated in Philotas's conspiracy. It was at this point that our author, Ptolemy, became one of the seven bodyguards, or Somatophylakes, who were also generals in Alexander's army. Also around this time, Perdiccas became one of the seven as well. As has been mentioned, these men were much more than bodyguards, holding positions such as general or, in the case of Hephaestion and later Perdiccas, chiliarch, which was a high-ranking position of commander and adviser.

Alexander continued his march toward Bessus in Bactria. He subdued the Drangians and the Gadrosians on his way. He also reduced the Arachotians to subjection and appointed a man named Menon to be viceroy over them. By this time, after marching through deep snow and other hard conditions, Alexander received word that the Areians had revolted yet again. Satibarzanes had returned with two thousand cavalry, which he had been given by Bessus. Alexander sent Artabazus, the Persian, as well as Erigyius and Caranus, two of the Companions, against Satibarzanes and ordered the viceroy of the Parthians to assist them. In the battle that resulted, the Areian forces held their ground until Satibarzanes was struck in the face with a spear and killed. Then they broke and fled.

Alexander marched on and came near what was called Mount Caucasus, in the Gandara region of modern-day Afghanistan. Here he founded a city that he named Alexandria. In all, Alexander founded some twenty cities that bore his name. The greatest of these was, of course, in Egypt. The Alexandria in the Caucasus would grow to become a relatively prosperous colony. After Alexander's death, it fell under the domain of Seleucus I Nicator, then was made part of the Mauryan Empire, and then passed through various powers until becoming part of the Parthian Empire.

Alexander crossed Mount Caucasus, where some Greeks believed Perseus had been chained by Zeus and where his liver was eaten every day by Zeus's eagle, only to have it magically grow back every night. This must have been a treacherous journey for the army because the mountains in this area are steep and barren, being part of what is today called the Hindu Kush. Bessus and the Persians who had gone along with his plan to capture then kill Darius and about seven thousand Bactrians were laying waste to the land on the other side of Mount Caucasus in the hopes of stopping Alexander's advance against them. But Alexander was undaunted. He pushed his men on, despite the snow and lack of provisions.

Bessus then crossed the river Oxus (today called the Amul Darya), burned the boats he used for his crossing, and withdrew to Nautaca in the land of the Sogdians. Bessus's followers were Spitamenes, a Sogdian warlord, and Oxyartes, with cavalry from Sogdiana, as well as a tribe called the Daans. Alexander marched onward and came to the largest cities in Bactria, Aornus and Bactra. He took these cities and left a garrison in the citadel of Aornus. He appointed Artabazus the Persian viceroy over Bactria.

Then he marched to the Oxus. This river is wide and deep and flows quickly enough that it was impossible for the army to

cross without some sort of bridge or boats. There was not sufficient lumber nearby, so it would have taken considerable time to
get what was needed to build a bridge so the army could cross.
Then someone struck on an idea, though our lost book probably doesn't mention who. The skins that the soldiers used as tent
coverings were sewn together with chaff, or dry animal fodder,
inside so that they were water tight. Then they were tied together to form a sort of floating bridge, which the army used to cross
the river in five days.

After crossing the Oxus, Alexander headed to where he
believed Bessus was, but he received word from Spitamenes and
another leader named Dataphernes that they would arrest
Bessus and hand him over to Alexander if the king would send
a small army and commander because they were holding Bessus
under guard and were waiting for the Macedonians. So it was
that Bessus found himself in the same position that Darius had
been in. He was betrayed by his allies, who were ready to give
him to the enemy. Our lost book would tell us that Alexander
now rested his army and sent Ptolemy—at the head of three
troops of cavalry, all the horse lancers, and a brigade of
infantry—to take Bessus. The following account almost definitely comes from our lost book, as it deals directly with
Ptolemy's actions.

Ptolemy somehow received word that Spitamenes and
Dataphernes, as Arrian puts it, "were not firmly resolved about
the betrayal of Bessus." So Ptolemy borrowed a strategy that
Alexander had employed in his pursuit of Darius, and left his
infantry behind with orders to follow him in a normal fashion.
He took the cavalry and advanced to an unnamed, walled village
where Bessus was with a few soldiers. Spitamenes and his men
had already left the village. Ptolemy surrounded the village with
his cavalry and issued a proclamation that the villagers would be
uninjured if they surrendered Bessus to him. The villagers
allowed Ptolemy and his men to enter. Arrian is no doubt copy-
ing or at least paraphrasing from Ptolemy's *History* when he says:

He then seized Bessus and departed; but sent a messenger on before to ask Alexander how he was to conduct Bessus into his presence. Alexander ordered him to bind the prisoner naked in a wooden collar, and thus to lead him and place him on the right-hand side of the road along which he was about to march with the army. Thus did Ptolemy. When Alexander saw Bessus, he caused his chariot to stop, and asked him, for what reason he had in the place arrested Darius, his own king, who was also his kinsman and benefactor, and then led him as a prisoner in chains, and at last killed him? Bessus said that he was not the only person who had decided to do this, but that it was the joint act of those who were at the time in attendance upon Darius, with the view of procuring safety for themselves from Alexander.

Alexander then ordered that the prisoner be whipped and then sent away to Bactria, where he was to be put to death. Aristobulus offers a somewhat different account of the capture of Bessus, in which Spitamenes and Dataphernes bring Bessus to Ptolemy and bind him naked in a wooden collar and betray him to Alexander directly. Perhaps this is an instance where Ptolemy has taken the opportunity to play up his own accomplishments. Instead of being a simple middleman, his account paints him as the hero who captured Bessus and conveyed him to Alexander appropriately. According to Curtius Rufus, Spitamenes brought Bessus directly to Alexander, the traitor's nose and ears were cut off, and he was crucified and shot through with arrows. It is almost certain that Bessus was not killed straightaway but was instead held prisoner for quite some time because he shows up later in our lost book's account.

After this, Alexander resupplied himself with the horses he had lost in crossing the mountains. He then went to Maracanda, the capital of the Sogdians, which was surrendered to Alexander. Then he went to the river Tanias, which Arrian incorrectly says originates in the Hindu Kush and empties into the Caspian Sea. In this region, the army was set upon by locals, who numbered possibly as many as thirty thousand. Alexander led a counterattack against these people and was wounded by an arrow through his leg, which broke the fibula. Still, he was able to capture the mountain on which they were encamped. Many were killed in the fighting, or died attempting to escape, and about eight thousand were captured.

Also around this time, sources other than our lost book speak of a massacre Alexander committed against a group of people called the Branchidae, whose ancestors had betrayed the Temple of Apollo near Miletus to the Persian king Xerxes. These people had gone with Xerxes and had settled in Sogdiana, where Alexander found them. As a punishment for their ancestors' betrayal, he massacred the entire population and tore down the buildings of the city. If this is true, it is reasonable to conclude that the lost book completely avoids the topic, as it might have seemed morally unsound to slaughter an entire population for a crime their ancestors had committed.

Now some envoys came from various tribes of the Scythians to treat with Alexander. Alexander sent some of his Companions away with them under the pretext of establishing peace with them but with the true intent to spy on the Scythians and determine the lay of the land so military expeditions could be made against them. He decided to found another city named Alexandria on the river Tanias that might be a base of operations for an invasion of Scythia and a stronghold against any incursions of outsiders. Arrian states that Alexander "thought that the city would become great, both by reason of the multitude of those who would join in colonizing it, and on account of the celebrity of the name conferred upon it." But this was probably true for every city that Alexander founded, since he envisioned multitudes colonizing all his cities, and they all bore his name.

It was at this time that the Sogdians killed the Macedonian soldiers garrisoned in their towns and joined together in revolt against Alexander. It was said that they even persuaded some of the Bactrians to join in the revolt. They massed together and planned to hold a conference in the city of Zariaspa, which seems to be another name for Bactra (Balkh in modern-day Afghanistan). Alexander had obviously misjudged these people. Had he treated with them differently or stationed larger garrisons or whole armies in these areas, perhaps the revolt would have been avoided. But Alexander was not the type of person to sit and regret things undone. Instead, he acted quickly.

eleven

PUTTING DOWN A REBELLION

A SACRED ZOROASTRIAN TEXT CLAIMS THAT SOGDIAN, OR Sughdha, was the second land created by Ahura Mazda, the highest god worshipped in Zoroastrianism, and it "was the plain which the Sughdhas inhabit. Thereupon came Angra Mainyu, who is all death, and he counter-created the locust, which brings death unto cattle and plants." This was the land that Alexander had conquered and that was now in open revolt against him. Alexander was told that the Sogdians were fortified in seven different cities. He gave instructions to his infantry to prepare ladders and assign them to each company, and he advanced to the nearest city, which was named Gaza. He split a portion of his army off and, under Craterus, sent it to Cyropolis, the largest city. Craterus was to surround the city, dig a trench completely around it, and set up some catapults and the like so that the inhabitants of the city would not be able to leave and aid any of the other cities.

Alexander found the Sogdian city of Gaza not at all like the city he had famously besieged before. This city had only earthen walls that were not very high. He ordered the ladders to be set up and his men to attack the city with speed. At the same time, the archers, slingers, and javelin throwers assailed the defenders on the wall. The walls were quickly cleared, and once Alexander's forces were inside, all the men of the city were killed. The women and children were, as Arrian puts it, "carried off as plunder."

It is highly likely that this comes from our lost book. It is a military action that Ptolemy would have been an eyewitness to. So why would it be okay to show Alexander ordering the slaughter of every man in this Sogdian city and the carting off of women and children as plunder, but it was not okay for Ptolemy to mention the massacre of the Branchidae? Simply put, because one is the brutal reality of warfare in the ancient world—men were killed, women and children were sold into slavery—while the other is a massacre as punishment for crimes of ancestors. Ptolemy was reading his audience. He knew that Greeks around the world would not fault Alexander for punishing a people who were in open revolt against him, but they might not forgive punishing a people for a crime their ancestors had committed.

After Gaza was taken, Alexander marched to the next city closest to it. This city is unnamed in Arrian's account, and Curtius Rufus gives no names for either of these cities, but it must have been similar in construction to Gaza, for Alexander took it by the same means and enacted the same punishment: all the men were killed, and the women and children taken as booty. These two cities were taken on the same day. The next day, Alexander took another city in the same manner. There remained two more cities that he hoped to take, but he feared their residents would flee once word reached them of the fate of the cities he had already destroyed. He sent ahead some squads of cavalry to stop anyone from fleeing. This was well thought out because people did begin to flee, and they were set upon by the cavalry and killed. Alexander eventually arrived with the rest of his army and took the remaining two cities on the same day, thus taking five cities in two days.

Next he went to Cyropolis, which Craterus had surrounded. Besides being the largest city in the area, Cyropolis was much better fortified than the other cities Alexander had recently taken. He ordered his siege engines to the walls and began to bombard them in the hope of breaking through them and creating an opening through which his army could assail the inhabitants. While this was going on, our lost book would tell us, Alexander realized that the river that ran through the city was not swollen by winter rains, so we can assume this took place during the warmer months of 329 BC. This meant that the channel for the river leading out of the city would provide easy access into the city. Alexander took his bodyguards (with Ptolemy among them), the shield-bearing guards, the archers, and the Agrianians and went secretly into the city, while those inside the city were focused on the siege engines battering the city walls. Alexander and his men opened a pair of gates and admitted the rest of his soldiers into the city. The enemy was taken by surprise, but they did fight back once they realized what had happened. The fighting was intense; Alexander suffered a violent blow to the head and neck with a stone, and Craterus was struck by an arrow. At this point, some eight thousand of the enemy were killed, while the remaining seven thousand sought refuge in the citadel. Alexander besieged them for one day, then they surrendered for lack of water.

Finally, Alexander went and took the seventh city. Curtius Rufus speaks of a city of the Memaceni, but it is unclear which city this was in the order of Alexander's campaigns. According to the lost book, this last city was surrendered without a fight. Aristobulus, on the other hand, states that the city was taken by force. However, Ptolemy's *History* is very particular on the matter, and that gives it a sense of validity, because he states that the men who surrendered were distributed "among the army and ordered that they should be kept guarded in chains until [Alexander] should depart from the country, so that none of those who had effected the revolt should be left behind."

Here we see how beneficial it is to try to recover our lost book. This detail speaks of a genuine memory that Ptolemy had, perhaps because he saw it as a wise decision on Alexander's part. This also shows that for Ptolemy, revolt was something that could not be tolerated and had to be punished with severe brutality. If a certain people revolted against Alexander, then Ptolemy saw no need to edit out the savage consequence. He might try to shift some of the blame if the revolutionaries were Greeks, as he did with Perdiccas and Thebes, but for the "barbarians," nothing was deemed too harsh.

As Alexander was taking these last Sogdian cities, an army of Scythians came together on the far banks of the Tanais. At the same time, Spitamenes, the onetime ally then betrayer of Bessus, was besieging the city of Maracanda. Alexander sent Andromachus, Menedemus, and Caranus with sixty Companion cavalry, eight hundred mercenary cavalry, and fifteen hundred mercenary infantry to stop Spitamenes. Over the whole expedition, he placed Pharnuches, a Lycian who was an interpreter, as Ptolemy and/or Aristobulus said, "Skilled in the language of the barbarians of this country, and in other respects appeared clever in dealing with them."

In twenty days, Alexander finished the wall around a city he had founded in the region, which would be called Alexandria Eschate, or Alexandria the Farthest. It was built at the site of the modern city of Khujand, Tajikistan. The wall was 3.7 miles long. Here he settled some of the wounded and retired Macedonians from his army. One wonders how much they cared to be settled so far from their homeland. Along with the Macedonians he also settled some Greek mercenaries and, as Arrian says, "Those of the neighboring barbarians who volunteered to take part in this settlement." Of course, this is a skewing of the truth; Arrian calls the process *synoecism*, which is a term for relocation that was often a euphemism for forced resettlement. Curtius Rufus states that prisoners of war were assigned to the city as well.

The Scythians remained on the other side of the Tanais, openly taunting the Macedonians. Alexander was still recovering from his head wound, and according to Curtius Rufus, he was barely able to speak, could not ride a horse, and was thus not able to lead his army. However, he resolved to cross the river and attack the Scythians. He was in the process of having the skins prepared to make another crossing when he offered sacrifice for the crossing. But when the portents were derived from the sacrifice, they proved unfavorable for his crossing. After some unknown time, he offered sacrifices again and was told by Aristander that the omens still portended danger for Alexander. On hearing this, he resolved to ignore the portents and undertake the crossing. Here, then, is a fine example of Alexander ignoring omens when they opposed his will. The skins were prepared, and the army was ready to cross. The military engines, catapults, and *oxybelai* (the last being precursors to the Roman ballistae), began to fire on the Scythians. One of these was able to strike down one of the higher ranking Scythians while he rode his horse on the riverbank and so bolstered the Macedonians.

Alexander, who it must be assumed had recovered somewhat from his head injury, led his army across the river. First across were the slingers and archers, who were ordered to shoot at the Scythians who had backed away from the riverbank. As his army came fully across the river, he launched some Grecian auxiliary cavalry and four squadrons of lancers against the Scythians. They received the attack, rode around the Greeks in circles, and wounded several. Next Alexander sent archers, the Agrianians, and other light troops mixed with cavalry against the enemy. Once they came into contact with the Scythians, he ordered forward three units of the Companion cavalry and the javelin men, with himself and the rest of the cavalry bringing up the rear and advancing in column. The Scythians were now not able to perform their circling maneuver. Thus the Scythians were routed, and they began to flee. A thousand of them died, including one of their chiefs, Satraces, and 150 were captured.

It was August 329 BC, and the day was hot, so Alexander's army did not pursue the enemy. Arrian claims that Alexander drank water from the Tanais and that the water was bad, which gave him diarrhea. For this reason he was carried back to camp, but one must wonder if his head injury had not fully healed and if this might have been why he needed to be carried away. Regardless, it proved that Aristander's prophecy had come true, for Alexander did fall into danger when he crossed the river. Here again we must conclude that our lost book pays special attention to omens and portents, and assumes that much of the future could be gleaned by looking at the present. The Scythians then sent envoys apologizing for the action and blaming it on a select few, saying it was not the will of their king to attack Alexander. Alexander was courteous in his reply and saw no reason to mount a full-scale assault into Scythia at that time.

Meanwhile, Spitamenes raised his siege on the citadel of Maracanda, as he had received word that Alexander's men, led by Pharnuches, were approaching his location. He retired to the northern reaches of Sogdiana. The Macedonians pursued him to the boundary of Sogdiana and the land of nomadic Scythians, not the same tribes of Scythians that Alexander had just concluded a peace with. Spitamenes gained some allies by these nomadic Scythians. He drew his contingent together on a flat piece of land near the Scythian desert. He did not openly attack the Macedonians, but he did not flee from them. Pharnuches mounted countercharges, but Spitamenes's forces were able to stay clear of these attacks because they had faster and fresher horses. Pharnuches's forces decided to give their horses rest and water and so went to the river Polytimetus.

Upon reaching the river, Caranus took his cavalry across it to get to a safer position. These had not been his orders, and it caused the infantry to follow across the river without knowing exactly what they were doing. Confusion commenced, and the enemy immediately saw the mistake. They fell on the Macedonians from all sides, cutting them down as they crossed the river and shooting arrows down on them while they were in the water. Every man of the expedition under Pharnuches died in the engagement. When Alexander received word of what had happened, he resolved to march against Spitamenes.

He took half the Companion cavalry, all the shield-bearing guards, the archers, the Agrianians, and the lightest men of the phalanx and marched toward Maracanda, where Spitamenes had returned to again besiege the men in the citadel. Alexander marched for three days, covering 170 miles, and came near Maracanda. When Spitamenes learned that Alexander was near-by, he fled as he had before. Alexander pursued him and came to the place where the previous battle had been fought. He stopped to bury the dead. He followed Spitamenes as far as the desert, then drew back and laid the land to waste. He killed any Sogdians and Scythians who were reported to have taken part in the attack on the Macedonians.

Now Alexander came to Zariaspa, to wait out the winter of 329 BC. Also arriving at Zariaspa were Phrataphernes, the viceroy of Parthia; and Stasanor, who had been sent into the land of the Areians to arrest the Persian general Arsames. Arsames was brought in chains along with Barzanes, whom Bessus had appointed viceroy of Parthia. Phrataphernes and Stasanor also brought along others who had joined Bessus in revolt. At the same time, several more bodies of troops came to Alexander from many quarters.

At this time, Arrian tells us, Bessus was brought before Alexander, having been kept as a prisoner since Ptolemy had captured him. Alexander accused him of betraying Darius and ordered that his nose and ears be cut off, and that he be taken to Ecbatana to be put to death in the council of Medes and Persians. Arrian takes this moment to comment on his distaste for mutilating the prominent features of the body as a custom. He goes on to state that he cannot approve of Alexander's taking on Persian dress and customs. Arrian states plainly that a man may accomplish much, but if he could conquer the world, "all these things would be no furtherance to such a man's happiness, unless at the same time he possesses the power of self-control."

Here is the Roman moralizing that seems to make up so much of our ancient sources on Alexander. So much of it, too, seems to be concerned with Alexander's taking on of Persian customs and dress. Our lost book doesn't appear to make much of this, and that would only make sense. Ptolemy, while remaining a Macedonian in many ways, took on much of what was expected of Egyptian rulers, such as dress and customs. His descendants even modeled earlier pharaohs and engaged in incestuous marriages. To an audience in the Roman Empire, this must have seemed an example of losing self-control, indulging in the lurid habits of foreigners. But to me, this seems to be just part of Alexander's personality as a leader. He began to view himself as the king of Asia, not just the king of Macedon, and so he adopted the customs and dress that would appeal to his subjects in that region. In fact, later on in his account, Arrian contradicts himself and states that he believes Alexander changed his dress and customs for political reasons and not as a sign of his loss of self-control. Just as he had identified himself with Ammon in Egypt and observed local religious rituals in just about every place he came to, Alexander was mindful of appearance. Ptolemy might have scoffed at first at Alexander's Persian change, but he must have eventually seen the logic behind it, because he would do something very similar in Egypt.

However, some were offended not just because Alexander adopted Persian dress and customs. At some point, and it is not clear when, he must have presented himself or allowed himself to be represented not just as a descendant of heroes and gods, but as a hero and god himself. There is little doubt that Ptolemy and the other Companions thought of Alexander as a hero, akin to Achilles and Heracles. Around this time, in 329 BC, coins began to be minted with Alexander's likeness, and often he was shown as Heracles. It is even said (though not by our lost book) that he would occasionally dress as Ammon, Artemis, Hermes, and Heracles with lion skin and club. It is impossible to say how much truth there is in this tale, just as it is impossible to know if Alexander truly believed himself to be a hero or god, but he did have good reason to think he was divinely protected. He was now twenty-seven years old and master of a vast empire. He had never lost a serious engagement with the enemy. He had been wounded many times and fallen ill, but he had come through it all a victor. The Persian monarchs were referred to as the King of Kings; the pharaohs of Egypt were gods among men. It is easy to see that Alexander might feel he was more than just the king of Macedon, because, of course, he was. It was his policy to take on some of the rituals and customs of those he conquered, so why would he not adopt their dress and assume the power afforded their rulers?

Of course, the idea that Alexander should be treated as a god may not have come from Egypt or Persia; it might have been introduced by Greeks. In one of his letters to Philip, Isocrates the great Athenian rhetorician stated that once Philip conquered Persia, there would be nothing left for him but to be a god. It had been Philip's plan all along to cross into Asia and make war on the Persians, but with his death that duty fell to Alexander, who did conquer the Persians. Alexander's tutor, Aristotle, in book 3 of *Politics*, states that a true king would be held as "a god among men" and to rule over him would be like trying to rule over Zeus. But of course, such language can be deceiving. There were certain ways, among Greeks at least, to honor someone as a god or a hero, namely to have temples built for them, sacrifices made in their honor, and games held in their name. There is no indication from our lost book that any of these took place while Alexander was alive. It is one thing to call someone a "god among men" as a sign of high esteem and respect, but it is another to sacrifice to him as a sign of worship and favor. Thus, if Aristotle ever expressed his opinion to Alexander that a true king would be a "god among men," it is not likely Alexander took it to mean that he would one day be an actual god. As we would say today, it was simply a figure of speech.

With the Isocrates letter, there are further considerations. For one thing, J. P. V. D. Balsdon, in his article "The 'Divinity' of Alexander," said the letter may have been a forgery written after Philip's death. It is also possible Alexander never read the letter. Furthermore, it seems to indicate that Philip would become a god after his death, not a living god. So we are left with the impression that Alexander did not, perhaps, abandon his self-control and fall victim to foreign whims, as Arrian would suggest, but that he took on the customs of the lands he had conquered and styled himself a "god among men." This would have been completely reasonable to Ptolemy, and he would have presented it, if he presented it at all, as part of Alexander's becoming the king of Asia and ruler of a great empire. It was truly in line with his actions up to that point, just as he was adopted as a son by Ada of Caria and hailed as the son of Zeus-Ammon in the Siwah Oasis.

twelve

THE DEATH OF CLEITUS THE BLACK

SOMETIME IN LATE 329 BC, OR MORE LIKELY IN 328, ANOTHER embassy of Scythians arrived to treat with Alexander. They stated that the Scythians were willing to follow any order Alexander might have and to bring gifts from their king. They also came to offer the Scythian king's daughter to Alexander to form a marriage alliance. If need be, the king also offered to come in person to meet with Alexander. At this same time Pharasmanes, the king of a people called the Chorasmians, came with fifteen hundred horsemen for Alexander's army. He told Alexander that his nation was confined by two other nations—the Colchians and the women called Amazons—and stated that if Alexander marched against these people, Pharasmanes would be a guide and supply the army with provisions.

Alexander was courteous to the Scythians but said he was not interested in marrying the king's daughter. He concluded a friendship with Pharasmanes and became his ally but informed the king that he was not presently interested in marching against the Colchians and Amazons. He introduced Pharasmanes to Artabazus the Persian, the viceroy of Bactria, and the other viceroys who were Pharasmanes's neighbors and then sent the king back to the Chorasmians. Alexander said then that his chief desire was to conquer the Indians, for when he had subjugated them then he would truly be the king of Asia.

One wonders who these Amazons were that Pharasmanes asked Alexander to conquer. The Amazons are, of course, the mythical women warriors who only tolerated females in their society and who cut off their right breast so they could better handle a bow. This particular account comes from Arrian, who is probably taking it from Ptolemy and/or Aristobulus. If it is Ptolemy, then it is probably an eyewitness account of what Pharasmanes said. If this is the case, then it is possible that Pharasmanes truly believed he was bordered by the Amazons. This, of course, could be the result of confused reports about long-haired warriors mistaken for women. Or there might have been a tribe with some women warriors that we are not aware of. It could be that some tribespeople were found and there were only women in the group at the time.

At this time, Alexander stated some of his future plans, and this information may be from our lost book. He declared that once he had conquered India, he would return to Greece and from there take his naval and military forces to the eastern end of the Black Sea, through the Hellespont and Sea of Marmara. Of course, Alexander was never able to fulfill this desire.

Alexander then marched back to the river Oxus. Many Sogdians had once again fled for refuge in their strongholds and were threatening revolt. While he was camped near the river Oxus, a spring of water and another of oil rose from the ground near Alexander's tent. Someone reported this to Ptolemy, who told Alexander. The king offered sacrifices in accordance with what his soothsayers indicated. Aristander, chief among the prophets, said the spring of oil was a sign of labors, and the labors would lead to victory.

Alexander crossed the river with part of his army and left behind Polyperchon, Attains, Gorgias, and Meleager among the Bactrians with instructions to guard that land in case the people began to revolt. He then divided the army he had taken with him into five parts. One was commanded by Hephaestion, one by Ptolemy, one by Perdiccas, one by Coenus and Artabazus, and the last by himself. They all then marched toward Maracanda, ending any resistance they met along the way. When they reached Maracanda, they stopped briefly. It may have been around this time that a tragedy occurred.

At this point it is unclear what source Arrian is using to relate this information. Given the facts of the tale, it seems improbable that Ptolemy would relate much of this story in his book, as it paints Alexander as a murderer if nothing else. Arrian relates that it was a specific holy day for Dionysus but that instead of offering sacrifices to that god, Alexander offered them to the Dioscuri, the twin brothers Castor and Pollux, also known as the Gemini. To celebrate the day, there was a party with much drinking. The discussion turned to the Dioscuri and the fact that one of the twins was a son of Zeus. This talk was meant to flatter Alexander and be suggestive of his own divine origins, with people saying that Castor and Pollux's deeds were nothing compared to Alexander's exploits. They then went on to compare him to Heracles.

One of those present was Cleitus the Black, one of the old guard who had fought with Alexander's father, Philip, as had Parmenion, who so recently had been killed on Alexander's orders. Arrian indicates that Cleitus did not conceal his distaste for Alexander's adopting the Persian style of dress and for the people who constantly flattered the king with comparisons to divine persons. He, probably like everyone else at this gathering, was drunk and could not sit by while people insulted deities or ancient heroes by saying they were nothing compared to a mortal man. He stated that Alexander's deeds were not as great or marvelous as they represented and were not achieved by him but by the collective deeds of the Macedonians. Alexander was annoyed by Cleitus's outburst, but the old soldier was not done. He went on to insist that Philip's deeds were still greater than Alexander's. He continued his tirade, more emboldened with each statement, reminding Alexander that he had saved the king's life at Granicus. He then put out his right hand and, according to Arrian, said, "This hand, O Alexander, preserved you on that occasion."

Alexander could take it no longer. He jumped up in a rage and had to be restrained by his closest companions, Ptolemy possibly among them. Cleitus continued his insults, so Alexander called his shield-bearing guards to attend him, but none of them obeyed in the confusion and heat of the moment. Alexander took this, as well, as an insult and compared himself to Darius put in chains by Bessus. At this point, Alexander was able to get hold of a javelin or pike and stabbed Cleitus, killing him. According to Arrian, Aristobulus does not say how the quarrel started but says that Cleitus enraged Alexander and was led away from the citadel in Maracanda by Ptolemy. Cleitus, however, could not control himself and ran back to Alexander and was struck with a long pike and killed.

If Ptolemy's *History* is Arrian's main source, then the uncited tale of Alexander drunkenly murdering Cleitus could be from our lost book. This seems somewhat incredible, because it does not cast Alexander in a good light. Of course, to an ancient Greek, Cleitus's murder would not have seemed as bad as it does to a modern reader. The most telling bit of information is that Alexander called his shield-bearing guards to him, as if he was about to order them to kill or arrest Cleitus, but they refused to obey his command. This shows that Alexander was not prepared to fight for himself and that he did not have command of his men at that moment. If this account is from our lost book, the only explanation for its presence is that Ptolemy did, in some ways at least, want to be truthful in his account. Perhaps the tale of Cleitus's death was well known, and Ptolemy simply hoped to set the record straight.

However, Ptolemy most likely didn't just end the tale with Cleitus's murder but continued with Alexander's reaction. After he realized what he had done, he immediately went to bed and began to call Cleitus's name, lamenting the loss and his own deed. He called for Cleitus's sister, Lanice, who had been Alexander's nurse when he was young. He bemoaned what he had done to her, she who had cared for him in his childhood. Her sons had died fighting for him, and her brother had died by his own hand. He called himself the murderer of his friends and would not eat or drink for three days. He paid no heed to his personal appearance and was deep in the grip of grief. Some of the soothsayers declared that this was the wrath of Dionysus because he had not sacrificed to the god on his holy day but instead had sacrificed to Castor and Pollux. Finally he ate some food and offered sacrifice to Dionysus. It is not clear if this comes from our lost book, but some ancient sources said that the sophist Anaxarchus came to Alexander and, finding the king lying down and groaning, laughed at him and asked him why he thought the poets of old had enthroned Justice alongside Zeus. He explained that it was because everything Zeus did was just and that it was the same with great kings—whatever they did was just to one and all. It was said that Alexander was greatly consoled by these statements. However it happened, Alexander was eventually assuaged and went on with his work at hand. Some historians think Cleitus's murder was not the result of wine and a heated argument but was a premeditated killing on the part of Alexander. Also, Cleitus was of that old guard who would seem to oppose the peace of Alexander's Greco-Persian empire.

The timing of Cleitus's murder is not completely clear, but it probably happened around the time Alexander sent Hephaestion away to create colonies in the cities of Sogdiana. He sent Coenus and Artabazus into Scythia because he believed

Spitamenes had fled there, while he stayed in Sogdiana and quelled the rebellions there. At this same time, Spitamenes and some Sogdian exiles fled to a place that the Scythians called the land of the Massagetae, where he collected six hundred horsemen and ventured into Bactria to a fort. He fell on the fort, killed all the soldiers stationed there, and kept the commander in custody. Spitamenes then approached the city of Zariaspa but resolved not to attack it. Some of the Companion cavalry had been left behind in the city because of illness, along with one of the bodyguards, Peithon, and Aristonicus the harpist. When these men heard that Spitamenes was near the city, they gathered themselves and eighty mercenary Grecian horsemen and pursued him. They engaged the Massagetae and killed some, but it turned out to be an ambush set up by Spitamenes, who then fell on them with force. Seven of the Companions and sixty of the mercenary cavalry were killed. Aristonicus was also slain in the action, as Arrian puts it, "having proved himself a brave man, beyond what might have been expected of a harper." Peithon was wounded and taken prisoner.

When the news of this was brought to Craterus, he made a forced march against the Massagetae, who began to flee as soon as they heard that the Macedonians were coming for them. Craterus caught up to this force and engaged it in fierce battle. According to Herodotus, the Massagetae's favorite weapon was the battle-ax, and "their arms are all either of gold or brass. For their spear-points, and arrow-heads, and for their battle-axes, they make use of brass; for head-gear, belts, and girdles, of gold." They were regarded as great warriors, and the battle must have been intense, but the Macedonians proved victorious. One hundred fifty of the Massagetae were killed; the rest fled into the desert and escaped.

According to Arrian, at this time Alexander relieved Artabazus the Persian of his viceroyalty of the Bactrians on the grounds of old age. It is believed Artabazus was beyond his ninety-fifth year. The position was supposed to be taken up by

Cleitus, but with his murder, Alexander instead chose Amyntas, son of Nicolaus. Coenus was then put in place of Amyntas over his own brigade plus the brigade of Meleager, four hundred of the Companion cavalry, all the horse javelin men, the Bactrians and Sogdians, and any others who had once been under the command of Amyntas. This force was left at Maracanda with instructions to protect the country and arrest Spitamenes if they were able to draw him into an ambush.

Spitamenes must have realized he was running out of options. Macedonian garrisons surrounded him, and no path to freedom was left. He decided to face Coenus directly and meet him in open battle. He was able to persuade some three thousand Scythians to join his growing army. Coenus learned of Spitamenes's movements and went out to meet him in force.

They met in battle and, yet again, the Macedonians were victorious. Of Spitamenes's forces, eight hundred died, while Coenus lost twenty-five cavalry and twelve foot soldiers. Spitamenes's Sogdianian and Bactrian allies deserted him and surrendered to Coenus. The Massagetae plundered the baggage of their allies and fled into the desert with Spitamenes. But when they heard that Alexander was on the march into the desert, they cut off Spitamenes's head and sent it to the Macedonian king in the hope it would keep him from pursuing them farther.

It was now winter 328–327 BC. At this point, we will take a short break from the narrative of Alexander's conquests and address the troubles of Callisthenes the historian. The reason we must break the narrative is that our main source for our lost book, Arrian, breaks from his narrative and tells the tale of Callisthenes in one long episode. It would be beneficial to tell this tale alongside other things that were happening at the same time, but it is not quite clear when the troubles first began for Callisthenes and when they ended. It is speculated that he died in spring 328 BC, a few months after the murder of Cleitus. If that is the case, we must travel back in time somewhat.

Callisthenes had been appointed royal historian for Alexander and traveled along with the king on his expedition into the East to chronicle everything that happened, making sure to show Alexander in a positive light. He was the great-nephew of Aristotle, and it is believed that through this connection he gained his appointment. What Callisthenes wrote has been lost, but it appears that it was overly flattering to Alexander. It survived long enough to coalesce into a text known as the *Alexander Romance*, a fantastical tale that was popular in the Middle Ages and led to some of the more colorful and contradictory legends surrounding Alexander, such as claiming that Alexander was the son of Darius, that he was a devout Muslim, that he explored the depths of the ocean, and that he was the son of an Egyptian pharaoh and magician. Perhaps it was the fact that Callisthenes was loose with his facts and that he was never able to finish his history that gave later writers the inclination to take it up and embellish it.

Regardless, Callisthenes was royal historian when Alexander began to adopt Persian dress and customs. The historian did not agree with this. In particular, he was averse to the proposed practice of *proskynesis*, the act of bowing before his king, which the Greeks believed was reserved for gods but Persian customs required be done for the Great King. The subject was broached at a wine party when Anaxarchus said Alexander was more deserving of the title of god than Dionysus and Heracles. His reasons were that Alexander had accomplished many great and mighty exploits, Dionysus was nothing but a Theban and in no way related to the Macedonians, and Heracles was an Argive and only related to the Macedonians through Alexander. So, he said, the Macedonians should confer divine honors on their king because there was no doubt he should be hailed as a god when he died. Wouldn't it make more sense, Anaxarchus asked, to honor him while he was still alive? Many people seemed to agree with this idea, but some were vexed by these statements.

Callisthenes spoke for all of them, it seems, when he responded, "O Anaxarchus, I openly declare that there is no honor which Alexander is unworthy to receive, provided it is consistent with his being human; but men have made distinctions between those honors which are due to men, and those due to gods." He stated quite plainly that temples are built for gods but not for living men, and that sacrifices are offered and hymns composed to honor the gods but not living men. He continued, saying the greatest distinction is that of prostration, which is given to gods but not to men. He added, "It is not therefore reasonable to confound all these distinctions without discrimination, exalting men to a rank above their condition by extravagant accumulation of honors, and debasing the gods, as far as lies in human power, to an unseemly level, by paying them honors only equal to those paid to men."

These quotes come from Arrian, and it is not clear if they are from our lost book. It seems unlikely that Ptolemy would credit Callisthenes with any reasonable arguments, given Callisthenes's eventual downfall and the fact that as pharaoh in Egypt, Ptolemy would have been given the honors of a god and so would probably agree with the arguments of Anaxarchus in this exchange. Also, Arrian tells us that he agreed with Callisthenes. It seems more unlikely that the Alexander apologist, Aristobulus, would have written this exchange, which could be seen as negative toward Alexander, especially since Arrian indicates that Alexander put Anaxarchus up to introducing the subject of giving the king divine honors at the wine party.

Callisthenes then continued in his long-winded response to Anaxarchus, saying it was wrong of him to even broach the subject because he was a Greek philosopher and instructor and should have remembered he was not speaking to the Persian kings Cambyses or Xerxes, but to Alexander the Macedonian, ruler by law, not by force. Eventually he turned to Alexander and gave him three choices: go back to Greece and compel "men most devoted to freedom" to prostrate themselves before him, stay where he was and make the Macedonians alone prostrate themselves before him (he seems to forget or ignore the fact that there were non-Macedonian Greeks in Alexander's army), or let the Greeks and the foreigners honor him in their own ways respectively.

Another time, Arrian reports, a golden cup was offered around, and those who prostrated themselves before Alexander were allowed to kiss him. It may seem strange to a modern reader, but this was a sign of familiarity that could be exchanged between any two people, even a soldier and his king. Also, there is no clear indication where the kiss was given—if it was on the hand, cheek, or lips. When the cup came to Callisthenes, he refused to prostrate himself and was therefore not allowed to kiss the king. It had already been determined at this point that the Macedonians were not required to prostrate themselves, but Alexander was rewarding those who performed the act in this instance. Callisthenes was heard to remark, "I am going away only with the loss of a kiss," meaning, perhaps, that he did not think it such a great dishonor to be rebuffed in this manner.

This scene most likely comes from Ptolemy and/or Aristobulus. If it comes from our lost book, then it is most likely intended to demonstrate the rude manner in which Callisthenes was conducting himself. To demonstrate that Callisthenes was not showing Alexander the respect and honor he deserved. And so, as Arrian puts it, "I surmise that this was the reason why such easy credit was given to those who accused him of participating in the conspiracy formed against Alexander by his pages, and to those also who affirmed that they had been incited to engage in the conspiracy by him alone."

thirteen

THE EMPIRE EXPANDS

Accoring to the ancient sources, Philip had begun a tradition of having young Macedonian nobles guard him while he slept and keep his horses. Alexander continued this tradition. Many scholars refer to these young nobles as pages, referring to the European custom dating back to the Middle Ages when a page was an apprentice squire, but it is not clear that these roles were synonymous. The young nobles of Alexander's court were probably young men in their mid- to late teens who served not only as royal guards and helpers but also as something like hostages to ensure the loyalty of their noble families. This is just part of the complex Macedonian political game that Alexander was at the heart of. Parmenion and Cleitus may have been killed for personal or strategic reasons, but their deaths were also politically expedient, as they helped usher out the old guard that might oppose Alexander's new Persian attitudes of royalty. The conspiracy of the pages and the ultimate death of Callisthenes can also be included among these political machinations.

Our lost book may have told a story that explained the origins of the conspiracy that would lead to the historian's death.

During a hunt, a young noble named Hermolaus struck down a boar that Alexander had marked for himself. As punishment, the young man was whipped in front of the other pages. He became enraged and told his lover, Sostratus, who was also a page, that he could not go on living unless he took revenge on Alexander. He then persuaded Sostratus and a number of other pages to join him in a plot to kill Alexander one night while they all protected him. Later in Arrian's account, Hermolaus gives as his reasons to kill Alexander the deaths of Philotas, Parmenion, and Cleitus, among others, and the "persianizing" of Alexander's court. These reasons seem more plausible than revenge, since it might be possible to convince young Macedonian nobles to kill a tyrant, but to expect them to throw away their lives to settle a personal vendetta seems somewhat far-fetched. However, it is likely that the second explanation is the one offered by our lost book, as Ptolemy would not have wanted readers to think the would-be assassins were just in their plot but that they were simply evil and prone to base emotions of envy and vengeance.

Whatever the reasons, the plotters were not able to carry out their act because on the planned night, Alexander stayed out drinking and did not come back to his tent to sleep. One of the conspirators broke his silence and told someone, who then told someone else, and it eventually reached our author, Ptolemy, who informed Alexander. The conspirators were arrested and promptly tortured, then confessed. Our lost book tells us that at this time, the pages pointed the finger at Callisthenes as being the mastermind behind the plot. According to Ptolemy, Alexander then had Callisthenes tortured and crucified, and thus the royal historian died. Aristobulus says Callisthenes died while in captivity, while other sources are silent on the matter. Whatever the case, it was a sorry end to the historian, but there is not much evidence to support the idea that he was involved in the plot. There is some evidence to indicate that he had connections with some of the pages, whom he was teaching, so perhaps this connection was exploited to provide a reason to kill him. Since he seemed to be so openly opposed to Alexander's deification and taking on of Persian customs, it seems particularly convenient that he should die when he did.

It is unclear whether the deaths of Parmenion, Cleitus, and Callisthenes led to more acceptance of Alexander's Persian dress or adoption of Persian customs. Our lost book is probably silent on whether everyone prostrated themselves before Alexander or if it was just the Persians and not the Greeks.

We return now to the winter of 328–327 BC and the furthering of Alexander's expansion. Alexander had rested his army and attended the duties of his empire. He sent someone to fetch Autophradates, the viceroy of the Mardians and Tapurians, because he had not come to Alexander though he was summoned. He sent Stasanor out as viceroy to the Drangians, and he sent Atropates as viceroy to the Medes because he questioned the loyalty of the current viceroy, Oxodates. He sent Stamenes to Babylon because the governor had died. And he sent some people back to Macedon to gather any recruits who waited there.

He waited until spring 327 BC to make his next move, which was directed at the so-called Sogdian Rock, a fort resting on top of a great rocky mound with precipitous drops on all sides. The remaining rebellious Sogdians were now holed up in this fortification and believed it to be impregnable. It was said they included the wife and daughters of Oxyartes of Bactria, who was one of those who had revolted against Alexander. It was believed that if this rock was captured, there would be nowhere left where the Sogdians could fortify themselves to continue their revolt. There was still a good amount of snow on the ground, and this made the approach that much more difficult. Those inside the fort were offered the chance to capitulate and were told they would be allowed to go peaceably to their homes. They laughed at this offer and suggested Alexander find some winged warriors to take the rock. This angered Alexander, so he offered prizes for those who could reach the summit, with twelve talents going to the first person at the top.

Three hundred men volunteered for the job and used iron tent spikes as ice picks to assist them in scaling the most dangerous and thus least-defended side of the fortress. They climbed the rock using rope and their spikes to keep themselves attached to the face of the cliff. Thirty of them did not make it to the top but died on the way. Once the others were at the top, they waved linen flags as a sign to Alexander, who then ordered a herald to go to the Sogdians and tell them that the winged warriors had been found. The rebels then saw the Macedonian soldiers at the peak of the mountain and assumed they were more numerous and heavily armed, so they surrendered immediately. Among those captured were Oxyartes's wife and daughters, one of whom was a young woman named Roxanna. She was supposed to be the most beautiful of the Asiatic women, besides Darius's wife, and it is said that Alexander instantly fell in love with her. Like so many things that Alexander did, there was political gain to be had from this relationship as well. The Sogdians had proven to be a very independent people, and Alexander had been constantly dealing with revolutions in that region since he had entered it. By marrying the daughter of one of the head war chiefs, he was gaining a loyal and powerful relative who might be able to ensure peace in the area. So Alexander treated her with respect and honor, and when Oxyartes heard this, he came to Alexander as a friend. He was welcomed into Alexander's court with honor.

It is probable that Ptolemy, in his *History,* did not make much of Alexander's engagement to Roxana, and the reason for this is simple. Roxana would eventually bear a son by Alexander after the king's death. This son, by Macedonian law, should have been heir to the Macedonian throne and all the lands his father had conquered. The Successors, including Ptolemy, eventually chose to ignore this claim, and one of them, Cassander, had Roxana and the young Alexander IV killed in 311 BC. This was not difficult to do because Alexander was not alive to confirm his heir and Roxana was nothing but a barbarian to the Macedonians.

According to Plutarch, Alexander married Roxana against the will of his commanders. Roxana was used, like Alexander's sister, as a tool for the Successors, and when she and her child were no longer useful, they were sentenced to death.

Our lost book does not seem to indicate that much time was spent in delaying the army after the capture of the Sogdian Rock, so Alexander marched on to another rock that he felt needed to be conquered. This one was called the Rock of Chorienes. Like the Sogdian Rock, this was a fortification surrounded by steep cliffs with one narrow passage leading to it. Alexander resolved to build up a road that he could lead his army on to besiege the fort directly. It is unclear how much time was spent on this operation, but it was never completed. First the men built ladders to descend into the ravine that surrounded the rock, then they began to build up from there. They worked ceaselessly, in day and night shifts, but were only able to make slow progress. Arrian does not state where he gets the details of the siege of the Rock of Chorienes, but it was probably a combination of Ptolemy and Aristobulus, because the first is mentioned by name in overseeing part of the operations, and it is believed Aristobulus was an engineer and so would have probably been involved in this construction. They reached a level where the archers were able to fire on the defenders, and this made the men in the fortress grow nervous. Chorienes, the war chief who commanded the rock, asked Alexander to send Oxyartes to treat with him. Alexander did so, and his soon-to-be father-in-law persuaded Chorienes to surrender the fort to Alexander and make a friendship with him. Alexander was honored by Chorienes's surrender and allowed him to continue to rule the land.

Next, Alexander returned to Bactria. He sent Craterus out with a force to stop two remaining rebels, Catanes and Austanes, who were commanding small armies of mountain people. Craterus met these men in battle and was victorious. Catanes was killed and Austanes was captured and brought to Alexander.

When Craterus was done, he returned to Bactria, and it is at this point, Arrian tells us, that the conspiracy of the pages and the death of Callisthenes happened. Thus we see the confusion as to when exactly Callisthenes died—328 or 327 BC. In fact, there is much speculation on the timing of events in Arrian around this time. Some suggest that the Sogdian Rock, also called the Rock of Arimazes, was besieged in spring 328 and that the tragedy of Callisthenes happened after this in 328.

It is believed that Alexander married Roxana in 327. As has been mentioned, our lost book probably doesn't give many details of the ceremony or the couple. We do not know if it was a Greek wedding or a Persian one, or something else entirely. Ancient Greek weddings took place in three parts and were representative not just of two lives being combined but of the combination of two families. Weddings often took place during January and during a full moon, as this was seen as lucky. The first day consisted of a feast at the home of the father of the bride, after which the bride would sacrifice things from her childhood like toys and clothes. The appropriate age for girls to marry was fourteen, while the appropriate age for men was thirty, after their military service. In Greek society, men had many more rights than women, such as the right to divorce for any grounds. Before the wedding ceremony, the bride prepared with a special bath. The ceremony itself, which took place on the second day, consisted first of a pact between the groom and the father of the bride, then the unveiling of the bride. Then the groom took the bride from her home to his. The final part of the wedding, which happened on the third day, was much like a modern-day reception, with food, drink, and music.

Alexander now left Bactria and headed toward India. He left Amyntas in Bactria with thirty-five hundred cavalry and ten thousand infantry. He crossed back over the Hindu Kush and came to one of the cities he had founded. Feeling that the governor he had put in charge was not doing a good job, he replaced him. This is another in a long line of administrative changes we have seen Alexander make in his empire. The idea that Alexander was simply a conqueror and would not have known how to administer his empire is patently false, for he was administering it as soon as he began to take foreign lands in his name. He placed Nicanor, one of the Companions, in charge of this city of Alexandria in the Hindu Kush. He also left wounded veterans there to colonize the city.

Next "[a]rriving at the city of Nicaea," Arrian says, Alexander "offered sacrifice to Athena and then advanced towards Cophen, sending a herald forward to Taxiles and the other chiefs on this side of the river Indus, to bid them come and meet him as each might find it convenient." Curtius Rufus says that Taxiles was actually the title of the king in this region and that his name was Omphis. Regardless, these chiefs came to Alexander and offered him their friendship and gifts of great value, including elephants. Though there were no clear borders in these days, one could safely say that Alexander now felt they had crossed into India. Here he split his army and sent a large force with Hephaestion and Perdiccas to march toward the river Indus and capture any places they passed on the way. Taxiles and the other chiefs marched with them. They were able to either capture or gain through capitulation every place they went, but Astes, the ruler of the land of Peucelaotis, affected a revolt. After a siege of thirty days, Hephaestion and Perdiccas took the city and Astes was killed. Sangaeus, who was an ally of Astes's but had defected to Taxiles, was then put in charge of Peucelaotis.

Alexander himself went to conquer the Aspasians. The account of this campaign in Arrian almost undoubtedly comes from Ptolemy's *History*, since Ptolemy took a leading part in these assaults against the Aspasians. Alexander took the shield-bearing guards, the Companion cavalry with the exception of those who had gone with Hephaestion, the regiments of foot Companions, the archers, the Agrianians, and the horse javelin men. He marched along a river called the Choes, which he then hazarded to cross. As he had done in previous instances, he let the infantry follow at its own pace while he took all the cavalry and some eight hundred infantry whom he had mounted on horses and force-marched them to the nearest city. It was there, according to information he had, that the locals had fled for safety. There is no mention of Alexander trying to treat with the Aspasians, so we are left to wonder if there was some information that led him to conclude that these people could only be taken by force and not capitulation. He routed the defenders who were lined up outside the city, though he was wounded by a dart in the shoulder. The dart was probably a missile with fletching like an arrow. It was either thrown by hand or with the aid of a spear thrower, which was a piece of wood or bone with a notch that allowed the dart to be flung at a higher speed than simply throwing it by hand. Ptolemy was also wounded in this engagement.

The city they were attacking, which is unnamed in Arrian's account, had two walls. At dawn the next day, they were able to take the first wall with ease. They began to scale the second wall and inflict damage on the enemy, who then turned and ran out of the city gates and toward the nearby mountains. The Macedonians killed many in flight and also killed all those they took prisoner because, as our lost book tells us, they were enraged that Alexander had been wounded. The next city he marched to then capitulated to him. Arrian, drawing from our lost book, then says, "He left Craterus there with the other commanders of the infantry to capture all the remaining cities which would not yield of their own accord, and to set the affairs of the whole country in such order as he should find most convenient under the circumstances."

Alexander now took a contingent of soldiers and marched to where the chief of the Aspasians could be found. After two days, Alexander reached this unnamed city. The inhabitants, learning of the Macedonians' arrival, set fire to the city and fled. Alexander pursued those who were fleeing and killed many. It is at this time that we hear an interesting story concerning

Ptolemy that we can safely say comes from our lost book. The story goes that Ptolemy saw the chief of these Indians on a nearby hill surrounded by guards. He pursued him, dropped from his horse, and engaged the Indian in a fight. The chief lunged at him with a spear, but his breastplate deflected the blow and Ptolemy cut through the Indian's thigh and dispatched him. He then took the Indian chief's arms and armor. This story has significance beyond just Ptolemy's heroic killing of an enemy. Like Alexander capturing Darius's bow and shield, Ptolemy's taking the armor from an Indian king gave him some claim to royal power as well. We must consider, then, that this is an exaggeration on Ptolemy's part to give himself some credentials for later becoming king of Egypt. There was more fighting with the Indians, and Alexander and Ptolemy proved victorious.

Next they came to the city of Arigaeum, which had been set on fire and abandoned by the inhabitants. Here Craterus met back up with Alexander's forces, and the king commanded him to rebuild and repopulate the city. Alexander then made for a spot where he had been told many of the remaining Aspasians had fled. He came to a particular mountain and encamped there. At the same time, Ptolemy had been sent out on a foraging expedition and had spotted a large number of fires in an Aspasian camp nearby. Ptolemy reported that there were more fires in that camp than in Alexander's. Alexander did not believe the report. He did believe, however, that the Aspasians had gathered into one large group. So he left part of his army encamped near the mountain and took a score of men to reconnoiter and possibly engage the enemy camp. Alexander then divided his army into three parts, with one under Leonnatus, one under Ptolemy, and the third under Alexander himself.

Ptolemy would prove to be right: there were a considerable number of Aspasians in the camp, and the fires were probably more numerous than the Macedonian army's fires. Given that this account almost definitely comes directly from our lost book, it is interesting to see this little episode. Ptolemy gives the report of the fires, Alexander doesn't believe him, and Ptolemy is proven correct. It is possible Ptolemy invented this exchange, but it is hard to see why he would. Although it shows Ptolemy as the one who is ultimately right, it shows Alexander doubting what Ptolemy says and in turn shows Alexander being wrong. None of this supports Ptolemy's ultimate goal of showing Alexander as deserving of power and Ptolemy deserving of power through Alexander. Since this account came directly from the *History*, it seems logical that this is an accurate account drawn from Ptolemy's own memories.

Alexander's force, divided into three parts, approached the camp and was soon spotted by the Aspasians, who came out to meet the Macedonians in battle. The Aspasians were emboldened by the fact that they had such large numbers and Alexander seemed to have so few. The forces converged, and the battle quickly ensued. Our lost book tells us that Ptolemy's men were not able to array themselves on level ground because the enemy was occupying a hill. So Ptolemy formed his men into a column and led them to the point where the hill was most assailable. The battle was heated and turned into a bloody contest. The Aspasians held their ground and proved to be fierce fighters, but ultimately they fell before Ptolemy's assault. Alexander was also victorious, as was Leonnatus. Ptolemy's *History* says forty thousand men and two hundred thirty thousand oxen were captured. Alexander picked out the finest of the latter and sent them to Macedon to till the soil.

This account is interesting because Arrian describes Alexander splitting his army into three parts commanded by Leonnatus, Ptolemy, and Alexander himself, yet only Ptolemy's division is described in detail. This surely came from Ptolemy's *History*, so we see more evidence that our lost book is at the very least autobiographical, though not a true memoir. We don't get a clear account of what happened to Alexander's division of the forces, because Ptolemy was not in that group. This is a good sign, because it indicates that Ptolemy reported in large part what he knew from experience and not just what he heard second hand. Of course, this is not always the case, as he seems to have reported on things that were happening with the enemy that he couldn't have experienced.

After this, Alexander took his army and marched toward the territory of the Assacenians, who were supposedly preparing for war against him. It was said that they had gathered some two thousand cavalry, thirty thousand infantry, and thirty elephants. Craterus now returned and brought along the more heavily armed troops as well as the siege engines. So now Alexander made for the Assacenians with the Companion cavalry, the horse archers, the brigades of Coenus and Polyperchon, the thousand Agrianians, the light-armed troops, and the archers. They came through the land of Guraeans, and crossed the river Guraeus, which proved difficult as the water was fast flowing and the round rocks were slippery and treacherous. When the Assacenians heard of Alexander's approach, they abandoned the thought of meeting him in open battle and dispersed to the various cities of the region in the hopes of finding defendable positions there where they might hold him off. First Alexander took his forces to Massaga, the largest of the cities in the region.

fourteen

THE BATTLE FOR INDIA

THE ARMY REACHED MASSAGA, AND WHILE THE MEN WERE pitching their camp outside the city walls, a contingent of Indian soldiers emerged and began to run toward them. It is said that Alexander hoped to draw this force away from the safety of the city walls and so he ordered the Macedonians to retreat to a nearby hill. The Indians perceived this as the Macedonians flee-ing and so continued their chase, but not in any clear formation. At the appropriate moment, Alexander ordered his men to turn around and advance against the enemy. This confused the Indians enough that they fell back and began their own retreat to the city walls. Two hundred of them were killed, and the rest made it back to the walls. While Alexander commanded an approach to the walls, he was struck in the ankle by an arrow, though it proved not to be a serious wound.

The next day, Alexander brought up the siege engines and easily battered down a portion of the wall, but the Indians put up a strong resistance and the Macedonians were unable to break through into the city. Alexander's forces were even stronger in their attack the next day, and a wooden tower was moved up against the wall. From here archers and catapults kept the Indian defenders back, but still they were unable to force their way into the city. On the third day of the siege, Alexander had a bridge built to cross over the breach in the wall. The bridge became overburdened and broke beneath the foot soldiers. The Indians saw this and began to assail the Macedonians with stones, arrows, and anything else they could hurl down on them. Some of the Indians even came out of the city to attack those who had been thrown into confusion by the collapse of the bridge.

On the fourth day, Alexander again tried to cross using a bridge. The Indians continued their strong resistance until at one point their ruler was struck with a bolt from an engine and killed. Because of this, and because their numbers were dwindling from the fierce fighting, they sent a herald to Alexander with terms of surrender. Alexander accepted their terms on the condition that the Indian soldiers join the ranks of his own army, as he thought they were brave fighters.

The Indians seemed to agree to this and came out and camped outside the city walls, but they camped far away from the Macedonians. It was said they planned to wait for night and then flee because they did not want to battle the Indians who were already on the side of the Macedonians. Alexander ordered his camp to be moved and surround the Indians who had come from the city, and when they started to flee, he attacked them and cut them to pieces. Now that the city had no defenders, he took it by storm and captured the mother and daughter of King Assacenus, who had died just before Alexander's arrival, according to Curtius Rufus. The ruler who was killed with the bolt must have been a relative of his. Our lost book would probably tell us that twenty-five of Alexander's men died in the siege.

From here Alexander sent Coenus to Bazira, believing that the inhabitants of that city would surrender once they learned that Massaga had fallen. At the same time he sent Attalus, Alcetas, and the cavalry commander Demetrius to the city of

Ora with instructions to blockade it until Alexander arrived with the majority of his army. The Indians of Ora made a sally against Alcetas's forces but were quickly defeated and driven back into the city. Coenus found that the people of Bazira would not surrender simply because Massaga had fallen and believed their city could withstand what Massaga could not. Upon hearing this, Alexander resolved to march to Bazira, but when he learned that some neighboring Indians were going to secretly enter the city of Ora and help defend it, he changed his mind. He ordered Coenus to fortify a strong position at Bazira that would keep the people from having free use of the land. Leaving a sufficient force for this purpose, he should then bring part of his force to assist Alexander at Ora. When the people of Bazira saw a large portion of the Macedonians leaving, they attacked the remaining force but were repelled. The siege of Ora proved to be easy, and with the first attack, Alexander captured the city, including the elephants left there.

When the people of Bazira heard this they despaired. They abandoned their city and made for a nearby rock or mountain plateau named Aornus, which had become a meeting place for all the Indians of the area. It was said of this rock that even Heracles could not take it, if it was being defended, so the Indians hoped, at last, to find a place where Alexander could not touch them. Aornus was said to be about twenty-three miles around and had a fine, flowing spring at the top of it. Only one narrow path led to the summit. So the Indians were understandably confident in their position. But the claim that Aornus could not be captured by Heracles only made Alexander that much more interested in taking it.

First, however, he had to secure the surrounding area. Arrian gives details that are almost certainly from our lost book. "He then made Ora and Massaga fortresses to keep the land in subjection, and fortified the city of Bazira. Hephaestion and Perdiccas also fortified for him another city, named Orobatis, and leaving a garrison in it marched towards the river Indus.

When they reached that river they at once began to carry out Alexander's instructions in regard to bridging it."

Alexander then placed Nicanor, one of the Companions, as viceroy over all the land on the west side of the river Indus. Arrian then tells us that through capitulation, Alexander obtained the city of Peucelaotis. A city with this same name was captured by Hephaestion and Perdiccas after a siege against the rebel ruler Astes, and it is not clear if this is the same city or another city with the same name. Regardless, Arrian says that a garrison of Macedonians under the command of a man named Philip was placed within this city. Then the army arrived at a city named Embolima, which was situated near the rock Aornus. Here Alexander ordered food and supplies to be gathered for a long siege campaign against the rock. He then took the remainder of his army and marched to the rock. While he was camped close to the rock, some Indian deserters came to surrender to him and told him of another approach to the summit.

He sent these Indians with Ptolemy, who commanded the Agrianians and a few other lightly armed foot soldiers. Yet again we can safely assume that Arrian's account is drawn directly from our lost book. Alexander gave Ptolemy "instruction, as soon as he had got possession of the place, to occupy it with a strong guard, and signal to him that it was held. Ptolemy proceeded along a road which was rough and difficult to pass, and occupied the position without the knowledge of the barbarians. After strengthening this position with a stockade and a ditch all around, he raised a beacon from the mountain, when it was likely to be seen by Alexander."

Alexander saw the beacon fire and on the next day marched his army toward the summit, but he was beaten back by the Indians and could go no farther. The Indians then turned and began to attack Ptolemy's position. A fierce fight ensued, but our author was able to hold his position, and the Indians backed down. Alexander then sent a letter in the night to Ptolemy with orders that as soon as Alexander made his assault the next day,

Ptolemy should make an assault as well, and thus their combined efforts might accomplish the task of taking the summit. The next day, Alexander marched up the path Ptolemy had taken. The Indians saw this approach and attacked. For the rest of the morning, the Macedonians and Indians fiercely contested the side of the mountain. Alexander's forces finally joined up with Ptolemy's, and the whole army assaulted the Indians' stronghold. But it was still unable to take the summit.

The area was covered with trees, so the next day, Alexander ordered the construction of thousands of wooden stakes. These were driven into the ground, and then a mound was built around them with the intention of providing a place where the archers and siege engines could fire effectively on the Indians. Arrian says that the building of the mound and the fighting at this spot went on for four or possibly five days, while Diodorus claims the fighting went on for seven. Either way it must have been another hard-fought battle, with part of the army building the mound and the other part fighting the Indians.

At this point, Ptolemy was acting as Alexander's second-in-command, since Hephaestion and Perdiccas were not with the army, and Craterus was back at the base of operations. So Ptolemy's account of these actions is probably the best one we could possess, except, perhaps, one written by Alexander. Arrian must have realized this, so we can be almost certain that many of these later accounts come from Ptolemy's *History*. Thus, to quote Arrian at this point is to quote our lost book, and if our goal is to get as close to Ptolemy's *History* as possible, then it is as if Ptolemy's words are bleeding through the surface of Arrian and we can easily make them out:

> On the first day his army constructed the mound the length of a stade [about six hundred feet]; and on the following day the slingers shooting at the Indians from the part already finished, assisted by the missiles which were hurled from the military engines, repulsed the sallies which they made against the men who were constructing the mound. [Alexander] went on with

the work for three days without intermission, and on the fourth day a few Macedonians forcing their way occupied a small eminence which was on a level with the rock. Without taking any rest, Alexander went on with the mound, being desirous for connecting his artificial rampart with the eminence which the few men were now occupying for him. But then the Indians, being alarmed at the indescribable audacity of the Macedonians, who had forced their way to the eminence, and seeing the mound was already united with it, desisted from attempting any longer to resist.

The Indians sent a messenger to Alexander saying they would surrender the rock under a flag of truce. Alexander granted them this but then learned that they planned to escape in the cover of night. So Alexander let them continue with their deceit but at the last moment ordered his men to fall on the retreating Indians. Many were killed, and many fell to their deaths on the sheer faces of the rock. Alexander, now claiming the rock as his own, offered sacrifices on the summit and ordered that a fort be built atop it. He then marched to the Indus, picking up a few stray elephants along the way.

Alexander next traveled to a city that Arrian calls Nysa. It is not clear which ancient city this refers to, if it is Nisa in modern-day Turkmenistan or another city. Yet it is known that Nysa was a mythical land where the young god Dionysus was raised. Also, during the Hellenistic period, Nysa was said to be the name of Dionysus's nursemaid. This city claimed to have been founded by Dionysus and named after his nurse, and when Alexander arrived outside it, their leader was sent to treat with him. At first he was taken aback because Alexander sat in his full armor in his tent, but Alexander bade him to enter and speak with him. The leader, who Arrian claims was a representative of an aristocracy that ruled the city, explained that they were founded by Dionysus and were a free people and so they asked that Alexander not attack them but leave them in peace. Arrian reports the representative's speech:

The Nysaens beseech you, O king, out of respect for Dionysus, to allow them to remain free and independent; for when Dionysus had subjugated the nation of the Indians, and was returning to the Grecian sea, he founded this city from the soldiers who had become unfit for military service, and were under his inspiration as Bacchanals, so that it might be a monument both of his wandering and of his victory to men of after times; just as thou also hast founded Alexandria near mount Caucasus, and another Alexandria in the country of the Egyptians.

Ptolemy would have heard this speech, so it is possible that it was recorded strictly from his memory. Because this happened after the death of Callisthenes, it is not clear if there was an official royal chronicler, but someone might have been taking note of this exchange, such as the royal secretary Eumenes. It was, of course, very clever on the part of these Indians to claim they were founded by a Greek god in the same manner that Alexander had founded cities of his own. At once they were flattering Alexander by showing him to be in the footsteps of a god and also they were claiming a kind of kinship to him, through the Greek Dionysus. They claimed to have proof of this connection in the fact that ivy grew around and in their city while it grew nowhere else in India. Alexander must have been convinced because he did not attack Nysa and accepted terms of peace as long as it provided three hundred horsemen to his army and one hundred aristocrats to be held, presumably, as guests and hostages. He appointed a man named Acuphis viceroy of the land of Nysaea and asked him to select the one hundred men. Acuphis demurred, asking how he could govern a land that had just had one hundred of its best men taken from it. Alexander saw the logic in this and so allowed that only the horsemen needed to be taken from the city.

Alexander then had a strong desire to go to the nearby mountain of Merus, which was thought to mean "thigh" to ancient Indians, though there is no clear evidence of this, and was thus connected to the tale of Dionysus being born from Zeus's thigh.

Ptolemy no doubt accompanied him on this journey. At Merus they found ivy growing in abundance, and everyone enjoyed it since it had been such a long time since they had seen ivy. Alexander offered sacrifices to Dionysus here and entertained a feast. Our lost book almost certainly doesn't hint that a drunken orgy unfolded on this mountain, but Arrian claims that other authors indicated that Alexander and his party acted the part of Bacchanals. This is a reference to the mystery cult of Bacchanalia, centered on the roman god Bacchus. By Arrian's time, the Roman gods Bacchus and Liber and the Greek god Dionysus were interchangeable, but in Alexander's time they would have probably known very little, if anything, of the Roman gods and their celebrations.

Next the army marched on to the Indus, where Hephaestion had built a bridge and a small fleet of ships was waiting. Also, Taxiles the Indian had sent two hundred talents of silver, three thousand oxen, ten thousand sheep, thirty elephants, and seven hundred Indian horsemen. According to Diodorus, Alexander let his men rest for thirty days at this point, but it would seem our lost book is silent on the matter. Alexander crossed the river and offered sacrifices on the other side. The first city he came to was Taxila, the largest city between the Indus and Hydaspes (now Jhelum) rivers, which is in modern-day Pakistan. Here he was met by the governor of the city, Taxiles, who would appear to be a different person than the previous Taxiles mentioned and so gives some credence to the idea that this was a title and not a name. But, of course, it is not uncommon for two people from the same region to have the same name—as was true of Macedonians named Ptolemy, Amyntas, and even Alexander. Several other envoys of nearby peoples came, offering gifts and friendship, and Alexander accepted them all. Here Alexander offered sacrifices and held games.

Here, also, he received word that King Porus of nearby Paurava was on the other side of the Hydaspes River and intended to stop Alexander from crossing. Alexander had all the vessels on the river Indus cut into pieces and carried by wagon to the Hydaspes, where they were reassembled and put into the water. He took his army, along with five thousand Indians under the command of Taxiles, and marched toward the river. The two armies spied each other from across the raging river. Alexander was determined to confuse Porus, so he split up his army into many smaller units and instructed them to range up and down the river so that Porus was uncertain when and where Alexander's forces would attempt to cross and had to split up his own army. One of these units was certainly commanded by Ptolemy, another by Hephaestion, and another by Perdiccas.

It was now late spring or early summer 326 BC, and the rainy season had begun. That combined with the melting of the snow in the mountains that fed the rivers caused the Hydaspes to be full and fast flowing. Alexander had stores of food brought up to give the impression that he might wait on that side of the river until winter, when the river would be more easily crossed. Alexander also ordered skins to be filled with hay, using the same trick he had employed in crossing other rivers. He practically covered the river with possible crossings and so kept Porus uncertain as to his intentions. Alexander then spread a report that he would wait until winter, in the hopes that this would reach Porus and confuse him even more. Alexander knew he could not cross the river directly into Porus's forces, since they outnumbered his two or three to one. Moreover, he assumed that the horses would not cross the river in the face of the eighty-some war elephants that Curtius reported Porus had and would cause nothing but chaos if they were put into the water to cross.

The skin bridges Alexander is supposed to have used must have been watertight to float on the surface of a river. No details are given, but there must have been planks placed across them so that they were something like a pontoon bridge over which wagons could roll and horses could be led.

Each night, Alexander and his cavalry rode up and down the river at various spots making as much noise as possible and raising war cries. At first Porus would lead his elephants to the side of the river opposite the noise, but as this happened many times, he began to regard them as nothing but feints and so stopped leading his elephants against a supposed nocturnal crossing. He simply posted scouts along the river in case of any such movements by the Macedonians. This is when Alexander made his move to cross. He found a bend in the river where the shore projected out into a point. It was heavily forested and provided much covering. There was an island across from this projection, and Alexander decided to cross onto this and then from there to the opposite bank. He left sentries along the way from his crossing to his main camp, which was over seventeen miles away. He left Craterus behind with a division of cavalry, several thousand Indian horsemen, and two brigades of the Macedonian phalanx. Craterus was ordered not to cross until Porus had left with his main force either to meet Alexander or to flee. Our lost book, being quoted by Arrian, might have Alexander ordering Craterus:

> If however Porus should take only part of his army and march against me, and leave the other part with the elephants in his camp, in that case you should also remain in your present position. But if he leads all his elephants with him against me, and part of the rest of the army is left behind in the camp, then you should cross the river with all speed. For it is the elephants alone which render it impossible for the horses to land on the other bank. The rest of the army can easily cross.

Alexander then arrayed his forces for the crossing. Between his crossing and Craterus he posted Meleager, Attalus, and Gorgias with the Greek mercenaries with orders to cross once they saw the Indians engaged in battle. He then took the Companions; the cavalry regiments of Hephaestion, Perdiccas, and Demetrius; the cavalries from Bactria, Sogdiana, and

Scythia; the Daan horse archers; the shield-bearing guards; the brigades of Cleitus and Coenus; the archers; and the Agrianians and marched secretly to the shore and then across the pontoon bridge to the island. There was a terrible storm that night, so they crossed not only in the cover of the woods but also the rain and clouds. They then crossed from the island onto what they thought was the mainland, but found it to be a large island that still cut them off from the opposite shore by a fast-flowing stream that had swelled because of the rains. By daybreak the rain had calmed, so Alexander, with Ptolemy by his side, crossed this stream with the water rising to the men's chests and the horses just keeping their heads above the waterline. Coming out of the river, Alexander began to array his forces.

First he placed a choice selection of his cavalry on his right wing, and in front of these he placed the horse archers. Next to the cavalry he placed the infantry with the royal shield-bearing guards under the command of Seleucus, who would go on to be one of the Successors and become king of Syria, creating one of the largest and most powerful kingdoms in the Hellenistic age. Next to these he placed the foot guard and the rest of the shield-bearing guard. At each side of his phalanx he placed archers, Agrianians, and javelin throwers. He had about six thousand infantry and five thousand cavalry. At this point, Arrian says that Aristobulus claims Porus's son arrived with a few chariots but was easily bested by Alexander. Arrian says other writers "say that a battle took place between the Indians, who came with the son of Porus, and Alexander at the head of his cavalry when the passage [of the river] had been effected, that the son of Porus came with a greater force, that Alexander himself was wounded by him, and that his horse Bucephalus, of which he was exceedingly fond, was killed, being wounded like his master by the son of Porus. But Ptolemy, son of Lagus, with whom I agree, gives a different account."

Our lost book says Porus's son arrived with two thousand cavalry and 120 chariots to face Alexander after he had finished his crossing of the last river. First Alexander sent the horse archers against the Indian force, followed by his cavalry, then his infantry, as he believed Porus had arrived with his whole army. But as soon as he determined the actual number of Indians facing him, he immediately ordered a rapid assault with the cavalry around him. The Indians fell before the charge, and Porus's son was one of four hundred killed. The chariots were captured, as they proved to be useless in the muddy soil. Porus received word that Alexander was approaching him and that his son had been killed. He delayed for a moment, unsure how to proceed because he saw Craterus's forces preparing to cross the river directly opposite him. Our lost book says he then took his full force, except a few elephants and a small number of men, and marched toward Alexander.

Arrian says that Porus had four thousand cavalry, three hundred chariots, two hundred elephants, and around thirty thousand infantry. He found a spot where the ground seemed to favor him, as it was hard-packed sand and not mud. He placed his elephants in front with about a hundred feet between them, assuming they would frighten the Macedonians and their horses and that no one would go between the elephants. He placed his infantry just behind, between, and on both sides of the elephants and his cavalry on the far wings on either side of these.

When Alexander saw the Indians thus arrayed, he slowed his advance to allow the infantry to catch up to the cavalry and also to give his soldiers a rest so they were not advancing against the enemy while exhausted. Alexander resolved not to attack the Indians head-on and thus face the elephants directly, and he knew that he outnumbered the Indians in cavalry and thought to push the attack there. Since Ptolemy was surely in a lead role in this battle, we can safely assume that Arrian drew directly from our lost book. So I will let Ptolemy continue:

> He [Alexander] took the greater part of [the cavalry], and marched along against the left wing of the enemy for the purpose of making an attack in this direction. Against the right

wing he sent Coenus with his own regiment of cavalry and that of Demetrius, with instructions to keep close behind the barbarians when they, seeing the dense mass of cavalry opposed them, should ride out to fight them.

Seleucus, Antigenes, and Tauron were ordered to advance with the infantry in phalanx formation but not engage until they saw the enemy's cavalry and infantry thrown into disorder by the Macedonian cavalry. He had his horse archers shoot at the left wing of the Indians while he advanced on that same wing with his cavalry. The Indians moved their cavalry to face Alexander's charge on their left; this left the field wide open for Coenus's cavalry to go around and behind the Indians and attack them at the rear. Thus the Indian cavalry faced attacks at the front and rear. This threw the Indians into confusion. The cavalry was then broken and fell back to the elephants, who tried to wheel around against the Macedonian cavalry.

At this time, the phalanx arrived and began to suffer heavy losses when facing the elephants, but it was able to hold its ground and attack the riders of the elephants and the beasts themselves. As Arrian puts it, "the action was unlike any of the previous contests." Seeing the Macedonians fall to the elephants, the Indian cavalry rallied and attempted another charge at Alexander. They were beaten back against the elephants and slaughtered. Now many of the elephant riders were dead and the animals wounded. The Macedonian army was pushing on them from many sides, and the elephants began to trample as many of their own men as their enemy. Eventually the elephants began to rush through the forces and leave the battle, backing away from the Macedonians, who were throwing javelins at them. Ptolemy, speaking through Arrian, continues:

Alexander himself surrounded the whole [Indian] line with his cavalry, and gave the signal that the infantry should link their shields together so as to form a very densely close body, and thus advance in phalanx. By this means the Indian cavalry, with the exception of a few men, was quite cut up in the action;

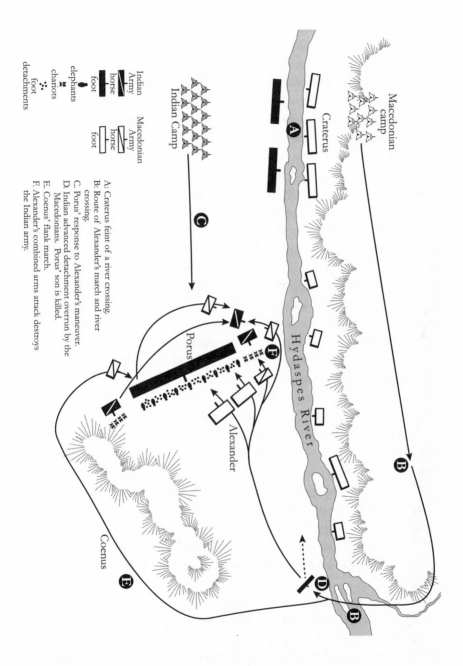

Indian Camp

A: Craterus feint of a river crossing.
B: Route of Alexander's march and river crossing.
C: Porus' response to Alexander's maneuver.
D: Indian advanced detachment overrun by the Macedonians. Porus' son is killed.
E: Coenus' flank march.
F: Alexander's combined arms attack destroys the Indian army.

Indian Army
horse
foot

Macedonian Army
horse
foot

elephants
chariots
foot detachments

Craterus

Macedonian camp

Hydaspes River

Porus

Alexander

Coenus

Map 5. The Battle of Hydaspes, 326 B.C.

as was also the infantry, since the Macedonians were now pressing upon them from all sides.

Diodorus says twelve thousand Indians were killed and nine
thousand taken prisoner, while Arrian says twenty thousand
enemy infantry and three thousand cavalry were killed. Of
course, Arrian could be including the captured in his total, as
they both might be considered casualties, so the numbers are not
so far off from one another. Those killed included two of Porus's
sons and Spitaces, the governor of that district. Also, Arrian
claims eighty elephants were captured. Arrian, probably drawing
from Ptolemy's *History*, puts Alexander's losses at eighty infantry,
ten horse archers, twenty of the Companion cavalry, and two
hundred other cavalry. Diodorus says 700 infantry were killed
and 280 cavalry. The total amount from Diodorus seems more
likely, as the infantry was said to have suffered in the face of the
elephants, but it is likely that the smaller amount would appear
in our lost book. This is just another example of Ptolemy giving
inflated numbers concerning enemies killed and deflated numbers for the Macedonian dead.

Porus did not flee the battle at the first sign of defeat, as
Darius had, but remained for some time and continued to fight.
Eventually he must have believed all was lost and did flee, but
Alexander did not want him killed. As Porus attempted to
escape on his elephant, which was probably injured, Alexander
sent various messengers to ask him to surrender. First he sent
Taxiles, but since that chief was a longtime enemy of Porus's,
Porus would not listen to him. Alexander sent a few others, but
they all failed. Finally he sent Meroës, an Indian and friend of
Porus's, who convinced the Indian king and led him directly to
Alexander.

Alexander rode out to meet Porus and was impressed with his
kingly manner and his great height, which was said to be about
seven feet. Porus met Alexander bravely and without any sign of
fear, and for this Alexander respected him. Alexander asked him
how he wanted to be treated, to which Porus is said to have

replied, "Treat me as a king." Alexander responded, "For my sake, O Porus, you shall be thus treated; but for your own sake you should demand what is pleasing to you." Porus responded that this was pleasing to him, so Alexander allowed him to remain king over the Indians he had been ruling and also added some more to his domain in the act. Alexander then founded a city where the battle took place and called it Nicaea, after the victory he had won there. He founded another city near where he had crossed the Hydaspes and named it Bucephala after his horse.

fifteen

A WOUNDED CONQUEROR

PLUTARCH REPORTS THE FAMOUS STORY OF ALEXANDER taming Bucephalus, before he became king. Philip had bought the horse, but no one was able to mount him until Alexander claimed he would be able to ride him. Philip let him try, probably hoping to humble Alexander. But Alexander, realizing the horse was afraid of his own shadow, pointed him at the sun so he could not see it. This calmed Bucephalus, and Alexander mounted him and rode away. It is possible that this story has some truth to it because Alexander was very fond of his horse and Arrian tells us that no one except Alexander was able to ride him. But the timing seems somewhat off given that the horse may have already been seventeen years old at this point. When Bucephalus was stolen in the land of the Uxians, Alexander threatened to kill the entire population until he was returned to him. The horse was promptly returned. Arrian, probably getting his information from our lost book, says the horse died of toil and old age after the Battle of Hydaspes, as he was about thirty years old.

Alexander buried the dead of the battle, sacrificed, and held games to honor the victory. He then marched on to the land of a people our lost book calls the Glausians. Every one of them came over to him on terms of capitulation. He took 37 cities in all, with about two hundred thousand inhabitants. He gave this land to Porus to rule. Envoys arrived from various kings and chiefs bearing gifts and offers of friendship to Alexander. Also, envoys came from another Indian ruler named Porus.

Alexander marched on to the river Acesines, which Ptolemy describes in our lost book. Arrian says it was the only river that he gave the size of, "stating that where Alexander crossed it with his army upon boats and skins, the stream was rapid and the channel was full of large and sharp rocks, over which the water being violently carried seethed and dashed. [Ptolemy] says also that its breadth amounted to 15 stades [almost two miles]; that those who went over upon skins had an easy passage; but that not a few of those who crossed in the boats perished there in the water, many of the boats being wrecked upon the rocks and dashed to pieces." So we see that our lost book not only covers the battles, the omens, and Alexander's actions, but also the journey itself.

It came to pass that the other Porus fled his land, as he was an enemy of the Porus now allied with Alexander. Alexander was determined to pursue the fleeing Porus. He sent Craterus and Coenus to forage the land as he marched to the river Hydraotes. He sent the ally Porus back to his homeland to gather elephants and troops and return to him. He sent Hephaestion into the land of the Porus who revolted to subjugate it and hand it over to the ally Porus. He crossed the Hydraotes with much more ease than the Acesines and marched on. Many of the people on this side of the river surrendered to him, though some tried to fight him but were defeated and forced to surrender.

At this point he received word that a tribe called the Cathaeans was preparing to fight him if he ventured into their land. He force-marched to meet them and after two days came to a city called Pimprama, which capitulated to him. He rested his army for a day and then marched on Sangala, where the

Cathaeans were situated outside the city on a hill with three rows of wagons surrounding them, acting as barriers. Alexander came to them and first sent his horse archers to ride around them and keep up a steady barrage of arrow fire, in order to keep the Indians from coming out and attacking. He then arrayed his forces in a battle formation. On the right wing he posted cavalry, shield-bearing guards, and the Agrianians. On the left wing he put Perdiccas with his cavalry and the foot Companions. On the far ends of each wing he placed the archers. As he was doing this, the rear guard arrived, and he spread these out into the rest of the ranks. The Indians jumped up onto the wagons and began to fire down at the Macedonians, but this accomplished little, and they were beaten back from the first row of wagons. They held their ground better now and were able to inflict some injury on the Macedonians, but the discipline of the phalanx proved unmoving and it beat them back again. They did not remain behind the third row of wagons, but instead fled into Sangala.

Alexander then settled his infantry around the city as much as he could and posted his cavalry around a shallow lake that came near the city walls. He suspected that come nightfall, the inhabitants would try to escape through this lake, and he was proven right. Many of the Indians were killed, but many escaped back into the city. Alexander strengthened his defense around the city and also around the lake. A few of the Indians in the city defected and told Alexander that many of the inhabitants planned to make another escape by way of the lake the next night. Alexander asked Ptolemy to command three regiments of shield-bearing guards, the Agrianians, and a group of archers at the lake where the suspected escape was to take place. Here, yet again, we are given Ptolemy's point of view in the proceeding action, so we must be further convinced that Ptolemy's work was autobiographical. This is not at all surprising and speaks to his attempt to present an accurate picture and not fiction that he is inventing from someone's point of view other than his own.

To help in confusing the would-be escapees, Ptolemy had wagons placed randomly in their path and had his men dig up mounds of earth to block their passage. Just before dawn, the Indians opened the gates by the lake and made a run for it. Ptolemy and his troops saw them, sounded the alarm, and attacked. The Indians, quickly realizing their mistake, turned back into the city, but five hundred of them were killed in the attempt. At this time, the allied Porus returned with five thousand troops and several elephants. Alexander readied his siege engines to finally take Sangala, but they were not needed. The soldiers managed to undermine the walls and take the city by storm using ladders. Arrian, most likely getting his numbers from Ptolemy, says seventeen thousand Indians were killed and seventy thousand taken prisoner. Less than one hundred of Alexander's forces were killed, though twelve hundred were injured.

It was summer 326 BC, and Alexander then marched on to the river Hyphasis. When he got there, he had planned to cross it and go on the Ganges River, conquering everything that lay in his path, but he was thwarted. Meetings were being held throughout the army, and many men began to declare that they would follow Alexander no longer. They had gone far enough; they had won enough glory; they wanted to turn back. Alexander gathered his officers and embarked on a long argument in favor of pressing forward. In Arrian's account, the speech is long and winding, but it contains some fine rhetoric. Alexander would have probably been a great speaker, able to stir his troops with a booming voice before battles and sieges. This speech might have been the most important Alexander gave, since this appears to be the first time his troops collectively refused to march with him. Their action is sometimes called the Mutiny at the Hyphasis, and while mutiny may not be the appropriate word, looking at Alexander's speech, one thinks it must have felt that way to him.

O Macedonians and Grecian allies, seeing that you no longer
follow me into dangerous enterprises with a resolution equal to
that which formerly animated you, I have collected you together into the same spot, so that I may either persuade you to
march forward with me, or may be persuaded by you to return.
If indeed the labors which you have already undergone up to
our present position seem to you worthy of disapprobation, and
if you do not approve of my leading you into them, there can
be no advantage in my speaking any further.

He went on to ask why, if they now found themselves the masters of a vast empire, they shrank from adding more to this territory? Were they afraid of the barbarians that lay ahead of them,
when all the other barbarians they faced had been defeated or
surrendered willingly to them?

Alexander continued, saying that to him a brave man's deeds
were only done when they were completely done, as long as they
led to glorious advancement. He added that if someone wanted
to know when their road would end, Alexander proposed to
cross India, which he said was not a far distance, and then come
to the Great Sea that circled the world. From there they could
sail back around Africa, which he called Libya, and pass the
Strait of Gibraltar, which he called the Pillars of Heracles. In
effect, he wanted all of Asia and Africa to be part of his kingdom, though his speech seemed to indicate that this would be
the empire of the Macedonians and Greeks as well, and not
Alexander's alone.

"But," Alexander continued, "if we now return, many warlike
nations are left unconquered beyond the Hyphasis as far as the
Eastern Sea, and many besides between these and Hyrcania in
the direction of the north wind, and not far from these the
Scythian races. Wherefore, if we go back, there is reason to fear
that the races which are now held in subjection, not being firm
in their allegiance, may be excited to revolt by those who are not
yet subdued."

He implored his audience to stand firm, reminding them that
they had accomplished things that their ancestors had done to

become heroes and gods. He spoke again of Heracles, whom they had bested by taking the Rock of Aornus, and Dionysus, whom they had surpassed by going beyond Nysa. He stated that the land they had conquered was theirs, the Macedonians and Grecian allies, and they were the land's viceroys. He also said that the money they had won was theirs collectively. He declared that if they marched with him to the end of Asia, then those who wished to return could do so and Alexander would lead them back, and those who wished to remain in this foreign country would be envied by those who went home. Alexander used many arguments and various reasons to ask his men to march on with him.

For a while no one spoke, and Alexander's words hung heavy in the gathering. Finally, Coenus, son of Polemocrates, spoke up. He said he did not speak for himself but for the bulk of the army, who were not present at the meeting:

> The more numerous and the greater the exploits have been, the more advantageous does it seem to me that some end should be put to our labors and dangers. For you yourself see how many Macedonians and Greeks started with you, and how few of us have been left. Of our number you did well in sending back home the Thessalians at once from Bactria, because you did perceive that they were no longer eager to undergo labors. Of the other Greeks, some have been settled as colonists in the cities which you have founded; where they remain not indeed all of them of their own free will.

It is impossible to say if this speech was all from Coenus or if he is presented as the mouthpiece of many arguments that were said by many different people at this meeting. In the last argument there is a hint at the peculiar nature of Alexander's position. He is a king, after all, but also the commander in chief of the Greeks, who are a free people, even if that freedom is only an illusion. The Athenians are free, in a sense, to cast off the rule of Alexander, but they know he would bring his full might down on them and punish them as he did Thebes. The Macedonians and Greeks—at least the men of a certain social standing—surely thought of themselves as free people who would not bow before anyone save a god. Alexander forced certain Greeks to be allied with him, forced them to colonize his cities, but could he force them to fight for him? The argument Coenus put forward was that he could, but he would not like the outcome:

> Do not lead us now against our will; for you will no longer find us the same men in regard to dangers, since free-will will be wanting to us in the contests. But, rather, if it seem good to you, return of your own accord to your own land, see your mother, regulate the affairs of the Greeks, and carry to the home of your fathers, these victories so many and great. Then start afresh on another expedition, if you wish, against these very tribes of Indians situated towards the east. . . . It is now your business to manage these matters; and other Macedonians and Greeks will follow you, young men in place of old, fresh men in place of exhausted ones, and men to whom warfare has no terrors, because up to the present time they have had no experience of it; and they will be eager to set out, from hope of future reward.

Coenus stated that these hypothetical fresh, young soldiers would follow Alexander with particular zeal once they saw the victories and spoils his current soldiers brought home.

According to Arrian's account, which comes from Ptolemy and/or Aristobulus, there was loud applause after Coenus finished his speech and even a few men who shed tears at his words. Alexander, however, was not so pleased with Coenus's speech. He broke up the meeting without a resolution and the next day said to his officers in anger that he intended to continue marching forward and any soldiers who chose to accompany him could, but the rest could return home, having abandoned their king among his enemies. Ptolemy would have been a part of that fateful meeting and probably heard Alexander's subsequent retort. It appears that he didn't add his opinion one way or another, or if he did, he didn't include it in his *History*. It would have been a delicate situation for someone in Ptolemy's position. He could very well have agreed with Coenus and the bulk of the army; having been at Alexander's side through it all, perhaps he had had enough. But as one of the bodyguards, a commander, and a friend of Alexander's, it would have been hard for him to be seen as criticizing his king in any way. If Alexander had continued marching, there is every reason to believe Ptolemy would have gone with him.

After Alexander lashed out at his men, he appeared to sulk in his tent for three days, allowing no one to enter and speak with him. He was apparently waiting to see if the opinions of his soldiers would change, but they did not. Our lost book tells us that Alexander offered sacrifices for crossing the river but the omens were unfavorable, thus hinting at the chance that these omens were given to suit Alexander, providing him with a reason to go no farther.

After this he gathered his commanders and Companions and made known that he would turn back and march home. The soldiers rejoiced. Alexander had twelve massive altars built, upon which he made sacrifices, and then held gymnastic and equestrian contests. He gave all the land up to the western side of the Hyphasis to the allied King Porus. He crossed the river Acesines and finally came once again to the river Hydaspes. Here he prepared ships with the intent of sailing down the Hydaspes to the Indus and finally out into what he called the Great Sea. At this point Coenus, who had so faithfully served Alexander and also been the voice of reason for turning back, fell ill and died. Alexander buried him with great ceremony, in appearance, at least, holding no ill will toward the man for speaking on behalf of the exhausted army. There is the chance that Coenus's death just after the turning back of the army indicates he was killed for his outspokenness.

According to our lost book, Alexander's navy amounted to eighty triremes and, including all the transports, numbered almost two thousand ships. Alexander and Ptolemy went with the ships down the river. Craterus led an army along the right bank of the river, while Hephaestion led a more substantial army with about two hundred elephants on the left side. According to Plutarch, Alexander had something like one hundred twenty thousand infantry and fifteen thousand cavalry combined. Our lost book seems to be silent on Alexander's total command at this point. If it was particularly large, as Plutarch suggests, it would fit with the apparent theme of underrepresenting Alexander's numbers in Ptolemy's *History*.

Alexander made the necessary sacrifices and poured several libations into the river to protect them on their journey. They set off down the river at an orderly pace. In Arrian's description we are told that the sound of so many oars in the water at the same time was unlike anything heard before, and perhaps this is from Ptolemy's own personal experience. They made their way down the Hydaspes to the point where it met the river Acesines. The joining of these rivers proved to be a perilous spot, and some ships and some of those aboard were lost in the tumultuous current. Alexander also received word that a tribe called the Malli and their one-time enemy, the Oxydraci, had made an alliance and sent their wives and children to fortified cities and were planning to prevent him from crossing into their territory. He resolved to meet this challenge with force.

He reunited with Hephaestion, Craterus, and Philip, a Macedonian commander. He transferred the horse archers, the elephants, and several infantry across the river and put them under the command of Craterus. He split the rest of his army into three parts. He ordered Hephaestion to take the first division and advance south five days ahead of his own command so it might capture any Indians that fled Alexander's advance to the east. He ordered Ptolemy to take another division and follow him by three days so that if any Indians fled from Alexander to his rear or to the north, they might be captured as well. He then marched east across a desert, covering some twelve miles in the first day, stopping for water, and then force-marched forty-seven miles the second day. He arrived at the small city of Kot Kamalia and surprised the population, who did not expect him to come across the desert nor, perhaps, to be marching during the rainy season in India, which was traditionally devoid of conflict. He found a large number of Indians actually outside the city walls unarmed. He killed many and drove the rest into the city.

Around this time, the alliance between the Malli and Oxydraci fell apart, and each tribe resolved to defend itself separately. After surrounding Kot Kamalia, Alexander sent Perdiccas with a force of cavalry and the Agrianians to the southeast with orders to blockade the city but not begin besieging it until Alexander arrived with his own force, fearing that some of the Indians might flee and warn other cities. He then began his assault on Kot Kamalia. The Indians could not hold the walls of the city against the Macedonians, so they went to the citadel, where they hoped to have a better chance of defending themselves. This proved to be unsuccessful, as the Macedonians closed in from all sides and eventually slaughtered some two thousand Indians in the citadel. In the meantime, Perdiccas had reached the city to the southeast and found it recently abandoned. He tracked down some of the refugees and slaughtered them.

Alexander then let his army rest until the first watch of the night, when he marched toward an Indian city (modern-day Atari), but first he crossed the Hydraotes. He pursued some refugees who were fleeing toward the city, killing some and taking some as prisoners. The rest escaped. He then dispatched Peithon against the refugees who were now holed up in a fortress. Peithon's brigade of infantry and two regiments of cavalry took the place with the first assault and then returned. Alexander took his forces to Atari, which suffered a fate similar to that of the first Mallian city they had taken, Kot Kamalia. The walls were abandoned, and the men fled to the citadel, which was then heavily attacked. Parts of the citadel's walls were undermined, scaling ladders were placed against them, and

Alexander was seen to be the first person to go over the wall. The rest of the Macedonians followed him. About five thousand Mallians were killed, and only a few were taken prisoner.

Alexander set off for the other Mallian cities in the area but found them all abandoned. He sent Peithon and Demetrius with cavalry and lightly armed infantry regiments to ride along the river with orders to kill any Mallians who did not surrender. Arrian states plainly that the results of this expedition were that "Peithon and Demetrius captured many of these in the woods and killed them." Thus it is not clear if they tried to take any prisoners or if they simply slaughtered all the Mallians they found regardless of their apparent orders. Alexander then learned that a force of Mallians had drawn up on the other bank of the Hydraotes in battle formation. He rushed ahead with only his cavalry force to meet this army, which our lost book claims to have been about fifty thousand in number.

Alexander came to the river and, without a pause, plunged in it to cross and attack the Mallians, who drew back at this initial assault. However, they quickly realized that Alexander had only his cavalry, so they turned back to fight. Ptolemy might have been riding alongside Alexander in this struggle, so it is possible that Arrian is quoting him directly when he writes:

> When Alexander perceived that their phalanx was densely com-
> pact, as his own infantry was absent, he rode right round their
> army and made charges upon them, but did not come close to
> fighting them. Meanwhile the archers, Agrianians, and the
> other select battalion of light-armed infantry, which he was
> leading with him, arrived, and his phalanx of infantry was seen
> not far off. As all kinds of dangers were threatening them at
> once, the Indians now wheeled round again and began to flee
> with headlong speed into the strongest of their adjacent cities;
> but Alexander followed them and slew many, while those who
> escaped into the city were cooped up within it.

Here we see Alexander leading his men in his normal intelli-
gent, though urgent, manner, and the supposed mutiny of his

troops seeming to do little to affect his command style. He surprises the Mallians with a rapid assault but doesn't let himself get caught in a hopeless battle before his infantry support arrives. In so doing, he won another clear victory. He then encamped around the city of Multan and began to besiege it. Once again the Indians quickly abandoned the outer walls and withdrew into the citadel, this one being especially large and well fortified. Alexander split his forces up, one under the command of Perdiccas and the other under himself. Alexander's command was the first to get within the city and reach the citadel, which it put ladders to and attempted to undermine. Once again, Alexander took to a ladder and, shield in hand, scaled it, and was the first to get over the wall. The shield-bearing guards were in such a hurry to reach the top of the wall that they crowded the ladders and broke them. The only other soldiers besides Alexander to make it to the top of the wall were the bodyguard Leonnatus, a distinguished soldier named Abreas, and the man who bore the sacred shield taken from the temple of Trojan Athena, Peucestas.

Alexander, seeing no other option, jumped down into the citadel and began to fight in hand-to-hand combat the Indians who came at him. In the fight, he was able to kill the leader of the Mallians there. Thus he kept the Indians at bay, though they continued to launch missiles at him. The other three soldiers jumped down to defend their king. Abreas was struck with an arrow in the forehead and fell where he stood. Peucestas and Leonnatus fought to protect Alexander, but an arrow hit the Macedonian king in the chest and went through his breastplate. Blood seemed to gush from the wound, and Alexander began to look faint and struggled to stand and defend himself. Our lost book, probably speaking from reports given later, tells us that the wound breathed air, indicating that the arrow had probably punctured a lung.

sixteen

HEADING FOR HOME

A CCORDING TO ARRIAN, OTHER ANCIENT HISTORIES CLAIMED that Ptolemy was there when Alexander was wounded and that he held his shield over the wounded king and was so given the nickname Soter, or savior, because of this. But Arrian clearly tells us that our lost history doesn't make this claim. In fact, Ptolemy states that he was not with Alexander on this occasion but was at the head of a different army, being sent to battle other Mallians in the region. When he was sent on this mission is not clear.

The Macedonians were frantically trying to fight their way into the citadel to rescue their king. Through various desperate measures, they were able to gain entry into the citadel and found Leonnatus and Peucestas, both wounded, attempting to defend Alexander, who lay on the ground, bleeding profusely from his chest wound. The Macedonians were able to get Alexander out of the fortress, carrying him on his shield. Then they began, in their anger, to slaughter the entire population, including women and children. There are conflicting reports on how the arrow was removed, and Arrian is not clear on what our lost book has to say about the subject. It seems that either a physician was on hand and he removed the arrow or that Perdiccas removed the arrow using the tip of his sword. Ptolemy, as has already been established, was not present, so anything he might have recorded was either taken from a different account or what he heard at the time. It seems that the initial report to make the rounds of the army was that Alexander was dead of his wounds, and so his soldiers began to grieve for their commander and king, but this report was eventually proven false. He lived, though his wound was severe.

Arrian reports that the army didn't believe Alexander would recover from his wounds, or believed he was dead but the generals and bodyguards were covering it up. There is no indication of where he gets this information, and even if it were from our lost book, it is hard to say how well Ptolemy would have known the mood of the average soldier. During the conspiracy of the pages, he was the one who eventually got word to Alexander about the plot, but this indicates that he had some connections with the Macedonian nobility, not the troops. So the mood of the soldiers in this matter is probably gathered from hearsay and speculation, as is often the case with the collective emotions of a large group of people. It is probably safe to say that some of the soldiers were incredulous about Alexander's recovery, otherwise the king would not have felt the need to show his troops that he still lived.

Alexander was carried down to the river around which the army was camped and put on a boat. Arrian says:

> When the ship bearing the king approached the camp, he ordered the tent covering to be removed from the stern, that he might be visible to all. But [the soldiers] were still incredulous, thinking that Alexander's corpse was being conveyed on the vessel; until at length he stretched out his hand to the multitude, when the ship was nearing the bank. Then the men raised a cheer, lifting their hands, some towards the sky and others to the king himself.

The shield-bearing guards came to the boat when it reached the bank of the river, with plans to carry Alexander back to his tent, but he ordered his horse to be brought. He then mounted his horse and rode back to his tent. There he dismounted and walked to the entrance. Many soldiers came forward and touched him and otherwise showed their love for him. One can assume that it must have taken all of Alexander's energy to put on such a display, but it showed to one and all that not only did he live, but he was likely to recover. There would have been an immediate effect on the camp, as if someone had lifted a terrible burden. Alexander lived and would continue to lead them home.

The army waited some time for Alexander to better heal from his wound, then it moved on. The Malli and Oxydraci sent emissaries to make peace with Alexander, gave him gifts, and offered him anything he might want in return for no longer bringing war on them. Alexander placed the commander Philip over these Indians as viceroy. Part of the army sailed down the Hydraotes into the Acesines, then stopped where the Acesines reached the Indus River. Here Alexander waited for Perdiccas to reconnect with the rest of the army. He handled the submission of local tribes and the placement of some soldiers to support Philip's governorship, and he founded a city at the convergence of the two rivers, this one known as Alexandria on the Indus.

Seemingly small matters followed: the moving of Craterus to the left bank of the Indus, the fortification of a city, the building of dockyards. Peithon was appointed viceroy of the general area. They entered the land of a king named Musicanus whom Alexander was prepared to subjugate by force. But Musicanus brought gifts and tried to placate Alexander, offering his land to the Macedonians. Musicanus was allowed to retain his kingship, although a garrison was installed in his capital.

All these details seem trivial compared to the great battles and hard journeys of Alexander's campaign, but they are almost all details that probably come from our lost book. That book, it seems, focuses largely on the administration of Alexander's conquests, from the position of troops during battle to the appointments of viceroys and the surrender of what seems like countless tribes and people. From the fact that Ptolemy doesn't place himself at Alexander's side when he is wounded and that he seems not to skip the more mundane details of Alexander's rule, we can begin to see that there is at least some attempt at verisimilitude. Ptolemy did not write an *Alexander Romance*, filled with flights of fancy. Perhaps he played up some things while he played down others. But even if he is not a perfect source, he is as close to reliable as one might expect for an ancient source on Alexander. Looking past Arrian, Ptolemy emerges as a flawed but capable historian.

Following the surrender of Musicanus, Alexander took the archers, the Agrianians, and the cavalry and marched against Oxycanus, the governor of the nearby country. He immediately took two large cities and captured Oxycanus himself. The other cities surrendered to him without a fight. He gave the booty of these cities to his soldiers but kept the elephants he captured for his army. He then marched against Sambus, the governor of the mountainous areas. When he approached the main city in this region, the gates were thrown open and the city was surrendered to him. Sambus's relatives told Alexander that the governor had fled, not out of fear of Alexander but because of the news of the surrender of Musicanus, who was an enemy of Sambus's. This seems highly questionable, but it is the reason that Sambus's relatives gave. Around this time, Alexander received word that Musicanus had revolted, so he sent Peithon with a force to capture Musicanus. Peithon went from city to city, destroying some and forcing the survivors into slavery or establishing garrisons and building citadels. Musicanus was brought before Alexander, who ordered him executed along with the Brahmin who had helped instigate the revolt. To the Greeks and Macedonians, Brahmins were philosophers because they were scholarly and concerned with the mind and soul. Brahmins have, of course, a long and fascinating history as part of Indian culture, being the priestly caste of Hinduism.

Alexander once again divided his army, having Craterus march on one side of the river while Hephaestion led a force on the other; he continued to sail down the river with part of the army. They eventually came to the mouth of the Indus, where they found the land empty, the inhabitants having fled at their arrival. They came to the city of Patala, which might be the modern-day Pakistani city of Thatta. It is possible that our lost book relates the detail that Alexander sent lightly armed troops after the fugitives and when they were captured he set them free, telling them that they would be free to come back to their home and work the land as they had. Many of them, it is said, returned. Alexander then ordered Patala's citadel to be fortified and wells to be dug so the people would have better access to water. These are just the sorts of details that Ptolemy would want to show to his readers: Alexander was not only interested in plundering but in ruling. There is every indication that Alexander planned for these places to be under Macedonian control for as long as possible. He was investing in these people as much as he was making war on them.

The journey down the Indus continued. Without local guides to help them navigate, some of the ships were damaged, but repairs were quickly made. Finally they reached the Indian Ocean. Some more ships were damaged because the Macedonians were not familiar with the effects of tide waters from a large ocean, but these ships were also repaired. Alexander then began to explore. He sailed out to an island and made offerings there. He sailed out farther into the ocean and made offerings to Poseidon, sacrificing two bulls and dropping some golden goblets and bowls into the ocean. He then sailed back up into the Indus Delta and found a large lake. He went aground, explored the land of the delta, and ordered more wells to be dug. He ordered dockyards to be built at Patala and at the lake he had found, intending to leave behind a large fleet.

It was 325 BC, and the season was not right for a sea voyage because there was no prevailing wind. It is important to note that Arrian probably relied on the record of Alexander's admiral, Nearchus, at this point in his history, as well as Aristobulus and our lost book. So it is especially hard to determine what bits of information come from what source. Ptolemy's *History* becomes somewhat murkier at this point. It is probably from Nearchus that we learn the admiral decided to wait for the winds and water to prove better for sailing. Alexander split his army in two, leaving half to travel with Nearchus by sea and the other half to follow him on an inland march back to Persia.

He then split the army following him in half again, leading the cavalry and lightly armed troops forward and leaving the rest behind under Hephaestion with orders to follow. He headed toward the land of the Oritians, an independent tribe who had not submitted to him. He took this land by force and killed or took prisoner all the Oritians. Hephaestion's force then caught up with him, and together the army marched into the desert of Gedrosia (the modern-day Pakistani province of Balochistan). There are varying opinions on why Alexander chose to march his army through this desert. He surely knew that the desert was large and formidable. There were stories of the Persian king Cyrus and others attempting to cross the desert and failing or losing scores of men in the process. One theory is that Alexander did it to punish his troops for the Mutiny at the Hyphasis, when the soldiers refused to march any farther. The other theory is that Alexander, hearing the stories of people unable to cross the desert, wanted to be successful where others had failed, to prove his greatness by performing another great deed. Our lost book, perhaps unsurprisingly, takes the latter view. That makes sense because besides not wanting to show Alexander as a vengeful and childish leader, the lost book would be providing the more accurate reasoning.

It is not hard to imagine that Alexander was frustrated and angered by his men when they refused to march to the Ganges;

our lost book even tells us as much. Yet if he had wanted to punish his soldiers, it would make more sense that he would do it in such a way that would allow him to get his way. He could have rounded up any leaders in this mutiny, had them executed, and forced his army to march forward. But he didn't do this, probably because he must have realized he could not lead such an army effectively. Coenus's words must have eventually made sense to him. Perhaps he was trying to punish his army by putting himself in danger and being wounded during the Mallian campaign, but then he would have had to orchestrate the breaking of the siege ladders, which of course he didn't. He could have forced his army through grueling marches in the campaign against the Malli, but he asked no more of them than he had ever asked of them; forced marches through harsh terrain were a key factor in Alexander's leadership.

Another key part of Alexander's character was a willingness to do what seemed impossible, just as he had taken the Rock of Aornus that Heracles had been unable to take, just as he had gone past Nysa where Dionysus had supposedly stopped in his own campaign. Alexander wanted glory—glory from winning great battles, from conquering a vast empire, and from doing those things that people claimed were impossible. Arrian tells us:

"Most of the historians of Alexander's reign assert that all the hardships which his army suffered in Asia were not worthy of comparison with the labors undergone here. They say that Alexander pursued this route, not from ignorance of the difficulty of the journey (Nearchus, indeed, alone says that he was ignorant of it), but because he heard that no one had ever hitherto passed that way with an army and emerged in safety."

The heat and lack of water caused the army to suffer greatly, as well as the beasts of burden that accompanied them. Almost all of the animals died or were killed for food when the provisions ran low. The number of men who died is somewhat unclear. Plutarch maintains that he lost three-quarters of his army to the desert. Horses and mules were slaughtered for food, but this meant sick and weak soldiers could not be carried, so many were left in the desert to die. At one point they were able to find a brook and camped near it, but the water soon flooded and carried off women and children among the camp followers, some of the beasts of burden still alive, and the royal baggage.

At this point, our lost book most likely relates a story that during a grueling march, when everyone was suffering much from thirst, some scouts went ahead and found a source of water. They came back and poured some into Alexander's helmet. He then poured it out onto the sand for all those around him to witness his sacrifice. Perhaps this story is a fabrication or perhaps it took place at another time. Curtius Rufus says this happened on the march in pursuit of Bessus, while Plutarch says it happened during the chase for Darius. If it did happen and did take place on this journey through Gedrosia, it undermines the idea that Alexander chose to punish his men since he was obviously attempting to inspire them to continue and was not still angry with them. Eventually they made it to the capital of Gedrosia, Pura, and there they were effectively out of the desert, their sufferings ended.

Next Alexander entered the land known as Carmania, which lies to the west of Gedrosia. Here Craterus rejoined him, bringing along the elephants. Alexander spent some time deposing certain viceroys and appointing new ones. He sentenced two to death because they had abused their power. He learned that Philip, the viceroy over part of the Indians, had been betrayed and killed, but that the Macedonian bodyguards had found those responsible and killed them. He was resupplied with beasts of burden to replace those lost in the desert. Arrian tells us that our lost book does not claim, as other ancient writers seem to have claimed, that Alexander traveled through Carmania lounging in a covered wagon, feasting, and listening to flute music, in imitation of Dionysus's legendary returning from India. It would seem our lost book simply indicates that he traveled as he had always traveled, on horseback and sometimes on foot, with his soldiers.

Aristobulus recounts that Peucestas, who carried the sacred shield and who defended Alexander when he was wounded by the Malli, then became the eighth royal bodyguard. We are given a list of all the bodyguards at this point: Leonnatus, Hephaestion, Lysimachus, Artistonous, Perdiccas, Peithon, our author Ptolemy, and the newly appointed Peucestas. As previously mentioned, the royal bodyguards were also the generals Alexander used to command various divisions of his army. Also, they were made viceroys, just as Alexander then made Peucestas the governor of Persis. Alexander then ordered Hephaestion to take most of the army, including the elephants, and march along the coast into Persis. He took the light infantry, Companion cavalry, and some of the archers and marched to Pasargadae, which was the capital of the Persian Empire under Cyrus, in the modern-day Fars province of Iran.

Once again we have Aristobulus's account on the matter, but it isn't clear what Ptolemy's *History* might have to say on the subject. The tomb of Cyrus is in Pasargadae, and Alexander discovered that it had been ransacked, with items stolen from it, and that the tomb was in disarray, the body having been thrown from the coffin. Aristobulus, the author of that other lost history that Arrian relied on, was ordered by Alexander to restore the tomb to its original condition, which he did. This is why many believe Aristobulus was an engineer, although it is possible he was simply a commander ordered to oversee this task. Alexander had the Magi, followers of Zoroastrianism, who were supposed to guard the tomb tortured, but they did not confess to any knowledge of who had robbed it and so were set free.

Alexander then went on to Persepolis, the Persian capital, where he had burned down the royal palace. Here Peucestas took on his role as viceroy of Persis, and to Alexander's delight, he adopted Persian customs and modes of dress, thus making it easier for the Persians he ruled to accept him. Peucestas would remain viceroy of Persis until 316 BC, when Antigonus One-Eyed deposed him as part of the struggles between the Successors.

Arrian tells us that various historians had various ideas about Alexander's plans at this point. Curtius Rufus, Diodorus, and Plutarch all seemed to have used the same source when stating that Alexander planned to sail around Arabia, past Ethiopia, around the whole of Africa, subduing these countries as he went, until he finally came back to the Mediterranean and would then surely be called king of Asia. We must remember that Alexander had no idea how large Africa was and that he would have viewed Africa as part of Asia. It is not clear that this is what our lost book claims. Arrian says that some authors claimed Alexander planned to go to the Black Sea, while others claimed he wanted to go to Sicily and challenge the burgeoning Romans in Italy, though there is no indication that Alexander had any knowledge of the Romans at all. But he probably would have known of the Carthaginians and might have been interested in making war against them.

Arrian sums up all this speculation nicely when he writes:

> For my own part I cannot conjecture with any certainty what were his plans; and I do not care to guess. But this I think I can confidently affirm, that he meditated nothing small or mean; and that he would never have remained satisfied with any of the acquisitions he had made, even if he had added Europe to Asia, or the islands of the Britons to Europe; but would still have gone on seeking for some unknown land beyond those mentioned. I verily believe that if he found no one else to strive with, he would have striven with himself.

At this time there was an Indian philosopher named Calanus who traveled with Alexander's army. He had become a friend of Alexander's, and the king was fond of him. Upon reaching Persis, Calanus fell ill and, not wanting to suffer the effects of ill health, told Alexander that he wished to take his own life. Alexander at first opposed the idea but then saw that it was truly what the Indian wanted and so allowed it. Ptolemy was ordered to build the funeral pyre. Calanus climbed onto it, and the thing was set alight. The Macedonians marveled at the Indian's calm manner as he was burned alive.

seventeen

DISSENSION IN THE RANKS

I T WAS 324 BC, AND ALEXANDER ADVANCED TO SUSA. HERE HE put a viceroy and his son to death because it seemed they had become tyrants, believing that Alexander would not return from India. Here also he married again, this time to one of Darius's daughters, Barsine. He also had many of his close companions married to Persian wives. Hephaestion married another of Darius's daughters, and Ptolemy was given Artacama, the daughter of Artabazus. In all about eighty Macedonians married Persian and Medes women. This, it seems, did not sit well with the Macedonians of the army. The group wedding was done in the Persian fashion, and this also probably rankled Macedonian sensibilities. It seems likely that our lost book explains these concerns of the Macedonians and that Ptolemy knew of them at some point. Yet it seems Alexander did not realize the breadth of the unease at first.

Alexander then sought to reward his soldiers by paying off any debts they had incurred during the campaign. He first set out to have a register drawn up of soldiers who owed money and then have those soldiers paid the amounts they owed, but the troops were hesitant to put their names on the register as they feared it was a means for Alexander to determine who had lived too luxuriously or beyond his own means and thus punish them. Alexander let it be known that this was not his wish and so set up a system where a man could come with a paper showing his debt and be paid without any names being written down and no record being made. He also gave particular rewards to certain soldiers he deemed worthy. In particular he singled out Peucestas and Leonnatus for protecting his life during the taking of the Mallian citadel and also the admiral Nearchus for bringing part of the army safely from India to Persia. He also rewarded the rest of the bodyguards, including our author Ptolemy.

Next the local viceroys came to Alexander with a force of new recruits numbering some thirty thousand, whom Alexander called Epigoni, or the offspring. These were Persian and Median youths who had been trained and armed in the Macedonian style. Alexander was most likely pleased with these newcomers, but the Macedonian veterans were not.

Alexander then traveled along the Tigris River and had some obstructions that had been put there by the Persians destroyed. The obstructions, called weirs, had been placed in the river to keep ships from traveling up the Tigris. Alexander then came to Opis, a city near modern-day Baghdad, where he drew the Macedonians together and told them that he was sending back home those who were no longer fit for service because of age or infirmity. For the Macedonians, this proved to be the straw that broke the camel's back. They saw it as his further attempts to abandon them and the Macedonian way of life in favor of foreign soldiers, customs, and modes of living. He had married his companions away to foreign wives, brought forth an army of Persians trained and armed as Macedonians, and applauded Peucestas for adopting the Persian dress and customs as viceroy of Persis. In their eyes, Alexander had gone too far. They voiced their offense to him and told him to dismiss all Macedonians from the army

He responded by ordering those who seemed to be leading the others in these arguments to be arrested, about thirteen in all, and put to death. While the rest of the Macedonians were horror stricken, Alexander climbed onto a platform before them and delivered an angry speech designed, it would seem, to change their minds by making them feel guilty. This struggle to combine the Macedonians and Greeks with the Persians was one Alexander never did resolve. His response this time is recorded by Arrian as a long, impromptu speech. It is hard to say if this speech truly happened and, if it did, how close it was to what we find in Arrian. There is little doubt that Ptolemy would have been there for such a speech, and so it is possible that this is drawn from memory. Yet, as we've already discussed, Ptolemy was probably not recording every word at the time but instead writing down the primary arguments as best as he could recall them.

Alexander's speech begins, "The speech I am about to deliver will not be for the purpose of checking your start homeward, for, so far as I am concerned, you may depart whenever you wish; but for the purpose of making you understand when you take yourselves off, what kind of men you have been to us who have conferred such benefits upon you."

First he listed all that his father, Philip, had done for the Macedonians, making them masters of Greece and no longer in fear of the tribes to their north. "He made you colonists of cities, which he adorned with useful laws and customs; and from being slaves and subjects, he made you rulers over those very barbarians by whom you yourselves, as well as your property, were previously liable to be carried off or ravaged."

He said everything Philip did was great but was nothing compared to what he, Alexander, had done for the Macedonians. He listed all the places that he took or were surrendered to him: Ionia, Phrygias, Lydia, Miletus, Egypt, Cyrene, Syria, Palestine, Mesopotamia, Babylon, Bactria, and Susa. "The wealth of the Lydians, the treasures of the Persians, and the riches of the Indians are yours; and so is the External Sea. You are viceroys, you are generals, you are captains. What then have I reserved for myself after all these labors, except this purple robe and this diadem? I have appropriated nothing myself, nor can anyone point out my treasures, except these possessions of yours or the things which I am guarding on your behalf."

It seems somewhat outlandish for Alexander to claim that the treasures were not his but really the property of the Macedonians. If these words were truly spoken, then it shows his skill at persuasive speech, for he was being highly political in the way he presented himself. All of these campaigns were done, he claimed, on behalf of the Macedonians and not, as some might think, for the glory of Alexander. Perhaps the soldiers didn't believe every word of what Alexander said, but they felt his anger and his disappointment, and it began to chip away at their hard feelings against him.

He continued his speech, saying that some might suggest he had not suffered as his soldiers had suffered. "Come now! Whoever of you has wounds, let him strip and show them, and I will show mine in turn; for there is no part of my body, in front at any rate, remaining free from wounds; nor is there any kind of weapon used either for close combat or for hurling at the enemy, the traces of which I do not bear on my person." He reminded them that he had celebrated their weddings with them and that their children would be akin to one another. He had paid off their debts for them. Anyone who died while on campaign died a glorious death, and their parents were treated with great respect and were exempt from taxes. He then commanded them to depart and tell their fellow countrymen that they had abandoned their great leader to the care of foreigners.

Alexander then went to a palace in Opis where he remained for two days, not allowing any visitors. Finally he saw the Persian commanders and began to give orders to rearrange his army under Persian leadership. When the Macedonians heard of this, they went to the palace gate and cast down their weapons as a sign of supplication to the king. Alexander came out to meet them, seeing that many of them were crying aloud and lamenting. One of them spoke directly to him, saying, "O king, what grieves the Macedonians is, that you have already made some of the Persians kinsmen to yourself, and that Persians are called Alexander's kinsmen, and have the honor of saluting you with a kiss; whereas none of the Macedonians have as yet enjoyed this honor."

Alexander replied, "But all of you without exception I consider my kinsmen, and so from this time I shall call you." With that, many of the soldiers came forward and gave Alexander a kiss.

This interaction between the Macedonians and Alexander shows the primary issue that he faced at the time: integrating his Macedonian and Greek soldiers with his Persian ones. He was looking for a peaceful coexistence of two unique cultures, which is a problem many leaders must face. Alexander's methods might seem crude, for instance, executing those who seemed responsible for friction between the groups and then making the Macedonians feel guilty to get them to change their hostile attitudes. Yet it was, at least temporarily, effective. His main concern about the Persians seemed to be that they would contest Macedonian rule, so he was certain to punish any viceroys who did not act as he wanted them to and punished revolts with extreme severity.

To celebrate the reconciliation, Alexander held a banquet that some nine thousand Persians, Macedonians, Greeks, and other nationalities attended. Then Alexander sent home any Macedonians who were injured or had come to retirement age. There were about ten thousand of these soldiers, and he sent them back under the leadership of Craterus. Craterus would die in 321 BC during a battle in which he was allied with Antigonus, Antipater, and Ptolemy against Perdiccas and Eumenes, part of the many wars between the Successors.

Alexander then marched from Opis to Media, reaching the city of Ecbatana, in modern-day northwest Iran. Alexander celebrated some gymnastic and musical contests. At this point, in autumn 324 BC, Hephaestion fell ill. There seems to be no indication from our lost book what form Hephaestion's illness took, as the focus seems to be more on Alexander's reaction. According to Arrian, and so possibly from Ptolemy, Alexander was at a gymnastic contest when he was told that Hephaestion was in an especially poor condition. When he went to see his friend, Hephaestion was already dead. There is speculation that Hephaestion was Alexander's lover, or had been his lover when they were younger but, as was common among Greeks, it turned to a close friendship when they matured, and this could be the case. It might have even been mentioned in Ptolemy's *History* but was edited out by Arrian, since the Roman view of homosexual relationships was much different than the Greek view.

Regardless of the details of their relationship, Alexander grieved deeply for his general and friend. Arrian states that various writers claimed various things about Alexander's actions following Hephaestion's death, but he doesn't say which writers said what, so we are left not knowing what might have come from our lost book. Arrian states that all the authors (we can assume Ptolemy is among them) agree on a few things, "that until the third day after Hephaestion's death, Alexander neither tasted food nor paid any attention to his personal appearance, but lay on the ground either bewailing or silently mourning; that he also ordered a funeral pyre to be prepared for [Hephaestion] in Babylon at the expense of 10,000 talents; some say at a still greater cost; and that a decree was published throughout all the barbarian territory for the observance of public mourning." Plutarch also says the pyre cost ten thousand talents, while Curtius and Diodorus say twelve thousand. Alexander also held gymnastic and musical contests that were greater than any he had previously celebrated, with over three thousand contestants involved. Arrian notes, perhaps getting this detail from our lost book, that many of these contestants would also compete at the games held at Alexander's funeral.

After a few months, Alexander finally came out of his mourning enough to embark on a campaign against a group called the Cossaeans, who lived in the mountains near the Uxians. They had previously avoided subjugation because they could retreat into the mountains, but Alexander was able to subdue them despite it being winter and marching over rough terrain. Ptolemy also led part of the army in this campaign. They then marched on to Babylon. On the way, many ambassadors from distant lands, such as the Carthaginians, Ethiopians, and Libyans, came to Alexander to offer friendship and declare him the king of Asia.

Arrian records various portents and prophecies concerning Alexander's end, but none of them clearly come from Ptolemy and our lost book, though the story of the Chaldeans may. As Alexander's army was approaching Babylon, he was met by a group of Chaldeans, a people from Mesopotamia who at one time ruled Babylon. They claimed that the oracle of the god Belus had proclaimed that Alexander should not enter the city facing the west, but should go around the city and enter in the opposing gate so that he would be facing east. Alexander questioned the motives behind this prophecy, thinking that perhaps the Chaldeans simply wanted to delay him because there was word that Alexander would rebuild the temple of Belus, which had been razed by Xerxes. The Chaldeans benefited from the temple remaining destroyed, for they were in charge of the property of the god while the temple was not built. Aristobulus says Alexander took their warning seriously enough to attempt to enter the other gate but found that his army would have to march through marshland to do so, and so it was impracticable. Therefore, he defied the Chaldeans' premonition and marched into Babylon facing west.

Alexander's fleet had met him at Babylon. He prepared to start an invasion of Arabia but first sent scouting vessels down the coasts while he went along the Euphrates River and a canal called the Pallacopas. On this voyage he founded a city that would come to be called Charax. Alexander sailed back to Babylon and was sailing through the marshes near the city when a strong gust of wind blew his wide-brimmed hat off his head, as well as a small band of metal that served as his crown. The hat fell into the water, but the small crown alighted in the reeds nearby. The sources are not clear, but someone, either a sailor or the commander Seleucus, jumped into the river and retrieved the diadem. Not wanting to put the crown in the water, the person put it on his head and brought it back to Alexander. Arrian says that most historians—again, we can assume this includes Ptolemy—say it was a sailor who retrieved the crown. Alexander rewarded him with a talent for his zeal and then promptly ordered him beheaded since no head should be allowed to hold the crown but Alexander's.

Back in Babylon, Alexander was met by Peucestas, with an army of twenty thousand Persians; Menander, with an army from Lydia; and Menidas, with a cavalry squadron. Alexander took these troops and reorganized his army, mixing Macedonians with Persians in each company. A Macedonian led each company and was seconded by another Macedonian, as well as a third, then came twelve Persians, then a final Macedonian. The Macedonians received higher pay than the Persians, and it was always a Macedonian who led, thus their smaller number was balanced by pay and position. One can see that this might have led to enmity from the Persians toward the Macedonians had Alexander led them into campaigns this way.

At this same time, Alexander received word from the priests of Ammon on whether Hephaestion could be worshipped as a hero. The answer was just what Alexander hoped to hear: Hephaestion would be considered a hero. Alexander sent word to Cleomenes, in Egypt, that great temples should be built in Alexandria to honor Hephaestion and that his name should be written on all the contracts of the city. Supposedly, Alexander told Cleomenes that he would forgive any crime Cleomenes had or would commit as long as he made sure these instructions were followed correctly. Arrian claims that this apparent blank check was in a letter to Cleomenes. But he does not say if he read the letter directly or if the story of Alexander forgiving Cleomenes for everything he had done or would do came from some other sources, so it is hard to say if Alexander actually wrote these things. If he did, it may have been one of the last letters he wrote.

eighteen

THE DEATH OF ALEXANDER

ARRIAN USES AS HIS MAIN SOURCE FOR ALEXANDER'S DEATH the *Royal Diary*. This would have been a seemingly daily account of Alexander's activity throughout his reign. It is presumed that this duty fell to the personal secretary Eumenes, or to Callisthenes before he was killed, but it is not known who was making entries in the *Royal Diary* at the time of Alexander's death. Arrian adds that Ptolemy's and Aristobulus's accounts do not vary much from the *Royal Diary*. On this we are forced to take his word.

The *Royal Diary* states that Alexander drank excessively at the house of Medius two nights in a row, May 31 and June 1, 323 BC. On the morning of June 2, he went back to his palace, took a bath, ate a little, and slept, as he was feeling feverish. He awoke later in the day and performed his customary sacrifices from a couch and then lay in the banquet hall. He gave instructions to his commanders, saying that those traveling by foot should be ready to leave in four days' time and those traveling with him by boat should be ready in five. Presumably this was in regard to his planned attack on Arabia.

Then he was carried to a boat, which took him across the river to a park where he bathed again and rested. June 3 he awoke, took a bath, and offered his customary sacrifices. He then lay in a covered bed, where he was visited by and talked with Medius. He ate a little and then went to rest. His fever raged throughout the night. June 4 he awoke, took a bath, and performed his usual sacrifices, then gave orders to Nearchus and others that the voyage would start in three days. June 5 he bathed and offered sacrifices, then gave instruction to have the fleet ready for the coming journey. In the evening he took another bath and was then "very ill," as Arrian puts it. This could mean that he was vomiting or that his fever once again got worse.

June 6 he was moved to a house near a swimming bath and offered his usual sacrifices. He was seriously ill but had his officers brought to him and continued to command them on preparations for the Arabian campaign. June 7 he carried out his sacrifices with great difficulty and spoke again with his commanders. June 8 he was gravely ill but still offered his sacrifices. He commanded that the generals should remain in the attendance hall, and the colonels and captains should remain before the gates. He was carried back into the palace. When his officers came to see him, he acknowledged them but seemed unable to speak. June 9 he was in a high fever throughout the day and night. June 10 his fever continued unabated.

In the evening of June 11, 323 BC, when he was just thirty-two years old, Alexander III of Macedon died in his palace in Babylon.

Some sources claim that when asked who would succeed Alexander to the throne, he replied, "To the best." Other sources suggest that he gave his signet ring to Perdiccas. Yet it doesn't seem our lost book makes such claims. From the moment of his death, through the time of the Romans, up to today, there has been widespread speculation on what killed Alexander the Great. One popular theory is that he was poisoned. Arrian himself gives voice to this theory in his *Anabasis:* "I am aware that many other particulars have been related by historians concerning Alexander's death, and especially that poison was sent for him by Antipater, from the effects of which he died." Moreover, Arrian says that these ancient conspiracy believers claim the poison came from Aristotle, the great Greek thinker and one-time tutor to Alexander, because Aristotle had also taught Callisthenes and presumably was concerned that Callisthenes's misdeeds would come back to haunt Aristotle. So, the theory goes, Aristotle acted preemptively. The poison, they claim, was given to Alexander by Iollas, Antipater's son and Alexander's cup bearer. Yet Arrian seems inclined not to believe such tales. Other supposed poisoners include any of his generals, one of his wives, or his supposedly illegitimate half-brother and author of our lost book, Ptolemy Lagides.

Our lost book holds no confession from Ptolemy that he killed his king and possibly half-brother, and the evidence supporting this theory seems uncertain at best. First, one must conclude that Alexander was poisoned, and there is no solid evidence that this was the case. Many of those claiming that Alexander was poisoned are using sources other than Arrian, Plutarch, Diodorus, and Curtius Rufus. Some of them even use bits of the so-called *Alexander Romance* to support their theories, or *The Journal of Alexander*, which many believe to be a later forgery. Ptolemy's *History* would have said nothing about poisoning, as it seems no one at the time considered this to be the case. In a way, it is almost surprising that the accusations of murder seem to have come out long after Alexander was dead and not right at the time of his illness. The Macedonians had already uncovered plots to kill Alexander. It was also well known that Alexander's father had been assassinated. So why didn't the people of Alexander's court suspect foul play right when he became ill or immediately following his death? Perhaps they did but didn't record it, or perhaps they simply missed the clues. Yet it seems just as likely that Alexander was not killed by poison but by something more mundane. Moreover, as the *Royal Diary* indicates, the key feature of Alexander's prolonged death was fever, and poisons do not usually cause a fever.

One recently proposed theory claims that Alexander was poisoned by ingesting a large amount of the plant *Veratrum album*, also known as the white hellebore. The toxicologists who proposed this, Leo Schep and Pat Wheatley, say this poison could have been in Alexander's wine on the nights he was drinking with Medius and that it would have been a protracted death highlighted by a fever. This fits nicely into what we know about Alexander's last few weeks and would seem to point the blame at Medius or someone in his household. Of course, this is just one of many theories.

Consulting information on the internet, the Wikipedia article on the subject, "The Death of Alexander the Great," lists as possible killers liver disease, typhoid fever, malaria, West Nile fever, acute pancreatitis, acute endocarditis, schistosomiasis, porphyria, and leukemia. All of these are possible, though some seem more likely than others. The argument for West Nile seems compelling, but the descriptions of Alexander's last days do not include certain characteristics of that illness, such as encephalitis; also, West Nile appears to be a relatively new disease. Malaria was (and remains) common, but the description seems to indicate a steadily rising fever over ten days culminating in death, and not the rise and fall of a malarial fever. To fit most closely with the description of the *Royal Diary,* which seems to be close to the description given by Ptolemy, the diagnosis would probably be typhoid fever. Of course, this is based on an unscientific description, so nothing is certain about the cause of Alexander's death.

From what we can tell, this is most likely where our lost book ends, with the death of Alexander. We know there must have been gymnastic and musical contests at the funeral, displays to rival anything that had been seen before. As has been stated, there was some discussion about where Alexander would be buried. It took two years to prepare his funeral procession, and in the end he was buried in a tomb in Alexandria. He was still there when the Romans defeated Ptolemy's descendant Cleopatra, and the new emperor, Augustus, is said to have placed flowers on the tomb and a gold diadem on Alexander's head. It is possible that Egyptian embalmers had worked on Alexander's corpse and so his remains were mummified when Augustus visited him. Sometime between that moment and the fourth century AD, Alexander's remains were lost. Perhaps they remain in Alexandria, under water, or perhaps they were moved and there is no longer a record of it.

At the so-called Partition of Babylon, Ptolemy received Egypt as his satrapy. Eleven years after Alexander's death, Ptolemy won a victory over Demetrius Poliorcetes in Gaza, part of the struggles of the Successors. To commemorate the victory, he had a stone engraved in the Egyptian style. It starts: "In the year seven, beginning of inundation, and the Holiness of Horus, the youthful, rich in strength, Lord of the diadems, loving the gods [who] gave him his father's dignity, the Golden Horus, the ruler in the whole world, King of Upper and Lower Egypt, Lord of both lands, delight of Ammon's heart, chosen by the sun, Son of the Sun, of Alexander the immortal, of the gods of city Pe [and] Tep, the friend. He being King in [a] stranger's world, as was His Holiness in Inner Asia, so there was a great Viceroy in Egypt, Ptolemy was he called."

This carving would have been done before Ptolemy wrote his book, and while it is obviously intended for a different audience than his *History*, the theme is similar. He exalts Alexander, here directly calling him a god, and then shows himself as Alexander's second in line, as if Alexander had placed him in the position of viceroy of Egypt, even though he clearly did not. Ptolemy's power comes through Alexander; this is the reason for evoking him in the carving, for bringing his body to and building his tomb in Alexandria, and for writing a history showing Alexander as that glorious victor and unrivaled king.

After the Partition of Babylon, things began to fall apart. Antigonus, governor of Greater Phrygia, fled from Perdiccas to Antipater, viceroy of Macedon, claiming that Perdiccas had designed to take all of Alexander's empire for himself. By this time Aristotle had died, just a year after Alexander, and the Greeks had once again been subjugated to Macedonian rule. Perdiccas sent Eumenes to stop the invasion of Antipater and Antigonus, while he went to Egypt to stop the person he considered his greatest rival, Ptolemy. As has been discussed, Perdiccas's attempt failed, and he was killed by his own men. Some historians say they were led by Seleucus, who would later come to rule Babylonia and eventually be king of the largest of the Hellenistic empires. Eumenes was successful in stopping the invasion—this is when Craterus was killed—but could not stop Antipater from leading a force south to assist Ptolemy. Eumenes's troops then turned on him, so his spot was given to Antigonus. Antipater became the new regent of Macedon, presumably to protect Alexander's mentally handicapped brother and his infant son.

In 319 BC, Antipater died and a new alignment was reached. Antipater's son Cassander allied himself with Antigonus in Asia Minor, Lysimachus in Thrace, and Ptolemy in Egypt. Polyperchon, whom Antipater had chosen to succeed him as regent, allied with Eumenes, who was sent back to Asia and was able to procure a small army of Macedonian veterans to his cause against Antigonus. He told his soldiers that Alexander had come to him in a dream and instructed that a tent be set up. Inside it should be a throne, and a crown and the arms and armor that Alexander was want to wear. Here commanders were to offer sacrifices and sit in council before the throne. This instantly won Eumenes the loyalty of his troops, and the instructions were carried out perfectly.

Farther to the east, Peithon, the satrap of Media, captured Parthia. The remaining satraps in the area had combined forces under the leadership of Peucestas. Eumenes was forced to move east in his fight against Antigonus. Peucestas and his ally Seleucus refused to acknowledge Eumenes as a representative of the Macedonian royal house. Eumenes tried his same trick with the tent and throne for Alexander on Peucestas and Seleucus, but it did not appease everyone. When Peucestas, Seleucus, and Eumenes combined armies and marched into Persis, Peucestas held a feast honoring the gods Philip and Alexander, with altars to each one set forth for offerings and sacrifices. Peucestas's apparent jealousy of Eumenes resulted in a critical moment when he disobeyed orders and both were captured and handed over to Antigonus. Eumenes was put to death, and Peucestas was held a prisoner, the rest of his life lost to history. Thus the chance for a unification of Alexander's empire under his heirs was lost, as Asia was now in the hands of the Successors, and through their struggles would eventually come their own kingdoms. In Greece, Alexander's heir and his widow, Roxanna, fell into the hands of Cassander, and it is presumed he had them killed, for they conveniently disappear.

It was then 311 BC, just after Ptolemy's decree concerning his victory in Gaza, and Alexander's empire was now carved up into pieces. Now these satraps began the transition of turning from Alexander the god to themselves as god-kings. They saw the fierce devotion and loyalty that could be given to a leader if he were worshipped as a god. Alexander's men loved him, and then they grew to worship him. The difference between love and worship is not so great after all. So the Successors began to think that instead of being satraps who answered to a royal house that no longer existed, they could form the royal houses themselves and be the god-kings at the heads of them. This included Ptolemy, the Roman emperors, and the countless other monarchs who came before and after and were either hailed as gods themselves or seen as divinely appointed.

In 306 BC, Antigonus's son, Demetrius, fought a naval battle in which he destroyed Ptolemy's fleet. He wrote to his father with the good news and addressed him as king. Antigonus replied with the same address to his son, so they both began to wear the diadem of royalty. Demetrius tried to attack Egypt directly but failed. He then turned his attention to Rhodes, which had declared itself independent on Alexander's death and had remained so during the struggles of the Successors. Cassander, Lysimachus, and Seleucus all came to the aid of Rhodes, but Ptolemy sent the most protection. When Demetrius was unsuccessful in taking the island, the Rhodesians asked the oracle of Ammon if they could honor Ptolemy as a god. The oracle replied that they could. They then set up a cult of Ptolemy and constructed a temple in his honor. They also called him *soter,* or savior. Antigonus and Demetrius's power grab culminated at the battle of Ipsus, in 301 BC, in which Antigonus was defeated. Cassander ruled Macedon; Lysimachus ruled Thrace and northern Asia Minor; Seleucus central Asia Minor, Persia, and all the land that Alexander had claimed to the east; and Ptolemy had Egypt and southern Asia Minor. However, Demetrius would eventually take Macedon from Cassander's son and become its king. It would stay in his line until the Romans conquered Alexander's homeland in 168 BC.

Around the time he declared himself king, Ptolemy sat down to write his history of Alexander. Perhaps he had a scribe there writing down his words; it is impossible to say. He would have had other documents at hand: a copy of the *Royal Diary,* the work of Callisthenes, and a copy of Cleitarchus's *History of Alexander*, which was highly popular. In fact, it is possible that Cleitarchus, who was from Alexandria, inspired Ptolemy to write his history because he sought to correct some of the errors that Cleitarchus made. This *History of Alexander* is also lost to time but would have been a source used by Diodorus and Curtius Rufus in their histories. Cleitarchus wasn't part of Alexander's army but probably got his information from Callisthenes; the diaries of Nearchus, the admiral, and Onesicritus, the helmsman; as well as the stories of the veterans living in Alexandria. Ptolemy, however, could rely on his own experience, and that is what makes his work so very important. There is little doubt that he felt uniquely qualified to write a history of Alexander, and it is interesting that he appears to be the only one of the Successors to do so. Perhaps they had none of the scholar in them, busy as they were ruling their kingdoms and waging their wars.

The question remains, what did Ptolemy's work ultimately say about Alexander? In his *Anabasis,* Arrian gives a brief description of Alexander's character. While he did rely on other sources, his main source was Ptolemy, so this can be seen as a type of review of the character of Alexander in Ptolemy's *History.* It reads:

> He was very handsome in person, and much devoted to exertion, very active in mind, very heroic in courage, very tenacious of honor, exceedingly fond of incurring danger, and strictly observant of his duty to the deity. In regard to pleasures of the body, he had perfect self-control; and of those of the mind, praise was the only one of which he was insatiable. He was very clever in recognizing what was necessary to be done, when others were still in a state of uncertainty; and very successful in conjecturing from the observation of facts what was likely to occur . . . very renowned for rousing the courage of his soldiers . . . very steadfast in keeping agreements and settlements which he made, as well as very secure from being entrapped by deceivers.

The Alexander who emerges from Ptolemy's *History* was brave, calculating, driven to glory, a man who could coldly order slaughter then turn around and show amazing leniency. His goals were sharply in focus and simple in nature. He wanted to conquer the world, but not just that. He wanted to rule what he conquered in peace. He hated revolutions as if they were personal betrayals, but he understood that some would be punished unfairly by his harsh treatment. He sought to expand his dominion as far as it would go, but he did not forget the mundane duties of rule or delegate the administering of his empire to others. He appointed viceroys to govern the various districts and then governed these viceroys himself. In war, he was of a singular brilliance. Ptolemy recognized it as readily as do the commanders of today, thus he was sure to include how troops were deployed in his history and also what losses were suffered. There is little doubt that Ptolemy exaggerated the number of the enemy and deflated the number of casualties on Alexander's side. He was undoubtedly biased toward showing Alexander in a positive light, but he could not have pre-

Bust of Ptolemy I Soter, 3rd century, B.C., at the Louvre Museum. (*Marie-Lan Nguyen*)

dicted the things that modern readers might respond negatively toward. So he tells us that Alexander sold whole populations into slavery and that he executed close friends based on circumstantial evidence.

Ptolemy provides the context that Alexander lived in because Ptolemy was much like Alexander, a Macedonian who would one day rule a kingdom in a foreign land. Unlike the Roman-era writers who chastised Alexander for adopting foreign customs and dress, Ptolemy understood the necessity for such gestures when ruling over a different culture. The average Macedonian soldier might have bemoaned the mixing of Persian soldiers with Greek, but by the time Ptolemy was writing his *History,* he was well aware of the difficulties with integrating two separate peoples, such as Greeks and Egyptians. If one were to ask Ptolemy whether he thought Alexander was a good or bad man, Ptolemy would have quickly answered that he was good. Not only was he good, but for Ptolemy—at least from his political point of view if not his personal belief—Alexander was a god, though he doesn't seem to labor this point. Or perhaps Arrian left those parts of Ptolemy's *History* out of his own *Anabasis.* But it seems Ptolemy presents Alexander as neither good nor bad, but great, glorious, and worthy of envy.

When we strip away the Roman view from the legend of Alexander, we are left with a clearer picture. It is still not a true depiction, but it is possibly as close to the truth as we are likely to get. Alexander strives to be among the great Greek heroes and succeeds despite a short reign and life. His main goal seems to be that he should be remembered for the ages. Obviously, he succeeded in that effort. Ptolemy, in writing his work, was striving to correct what he considered errors and provide his version of the deeds of Alexander. Despite his book being considered lost, he succeeded nonetheless.

BIBLIOGRAPHY

ANCIENT SOURCES

Arrian. *Alexander the Great: The Anabasis and the Indica.* Translated by Martin Hammond. Oxford: Oxford University Press, 2013.

Arrian. *Anabasis of Alexander and Indica.* Translated by Edward James Chinnock. London: George Bell & Sons, 1893.

Diodorus Siculus. *The Library of History,* vol. 9. Loeb Classical Library Edition, 1947. http://penelope.uchicago.edu/Thayer/E/Roman/Texts/Diodorus_Siculus/.

Herodotus. *Histories.* "Ancient History Sourcebook: Herodutus: On Libya, from *The Histories.*" www.fordham.edu/halsall/ancient/herod-libya1.asp.

Homer. *The Iliad.* Translated by Samuel Butler. http://classics.mit.edu/Homer/iliad.html.

Plutarch. *The Life of Alexander.* New York: Modern Library, 2004.

Quintus Curtius Rufus. *The History of Alexander.* Translated by John Yardley. New York: Penguin, 1984.

Strabo. *Geography,* vol. 1. Loeb Classical Library Edition, 1917. http://penelope.uchicago.edu/Thayer/E/Roman/Texts/Strabo/.

MODERN SOURCES

"Aristander, the Seer." Pathos.org. www.pothos.org/content/index.php?page=aristander.

Balsdon, J. P. V. D. "The 'Divinity' of Alexander." *Historia: Zeitschrift für Alte Geschichte,* Bd. 1, H. 3 (1950): 363–388.

Bell, H. I. "Alexandria." *Journal of Egyptian Archaeology* 13, November 1927.

Bevan, Edwyn R. *The House of Ptolemy: A History of Hellenistic Egypt under the Ptolemaic Dynasty.* Reprint, Ares Publishers, 1989. http://penelope.uchicago.edu/Thayer/E/Gazetteer/Places/Africa/Egypt/_Texts/BEVHOP/.

Bieber, Margarete. "The Portraits of Alexander the Great." *Proceedings of the American Philosophical Society* 93, no. 5 (Nov. 30, 1940): 373–421, 423–427.

Burke, Edmund M. "Philip II and Alexander the Great." *Military Affairs* 47, no. 2 (Apr. 1983): 67–70.

Cantor, Norman F. *Alexander the Great: Journey to the End of the Earth.* New York: HarperCollins, 2005.

Carney, Elizabeth. "The Conspiracy of Hermolaus." *Classical Journal* 76, no. 3 (Feb.–Mar. 1981): 223–231.

Chesser, Preston. "The Burning of the Library of Alexandria." eHistory Archive. http://ehistory.osu.edu/world/articles/article-view.cfm?aid=9.

Cunha, Burke. "Alexander the Great and West Nile Virus Encephalitis" response. *Emerging Infectious Diseases* 10, no. 7 (Jul. 2004). www.ncbi.nlm.nih.gov/pmc/articles/PMC3323347/.

"Death of Alexander the Great," Wikipedia, http://en.wikipedia.org/wiki/Death_of_Alexander_the_Great.

Devine, A. M. "Grand Tactics at Gaugamela." *Phoenix* 29, no. 4 (Winter 1975): 374–385.

Dodge, Theodore Ayrault. *Alexander.* Boston: Houghton, Mifflin, 1890.

Dollinger, Andre. "Ancient Egyptian Bestiary: Snakes." www.reshafim.org.il/ad/egypt/bestiary/snake.htm.

———. "Decree of the Satrap Ptolemy Lagides." www.reshafim.org.il/ad/egypt/texts/lagides.htm.

Easton, Matthew George. *Illustrated Bible Dictionary.* London: T. Nelson and Sons, 1894.

"Greek Weddings." Rise of Civilization. http://sites.matrix.msu.edu/anp363-ss12/2012/03/27/greek-weddings/.

Green, Peter. *The Hellenistic Age: A Short History.* New York: Modern Library, 2007.

"Gymnasium." *A Dictionary of Greek and Roman Antiquities.* Edited by William Smith. London: John Murray, 1875. http://penelope. uchicago.edu/Thayer/E/Roman/Texts/secondary/SMIGRA*/Gymn asium.html.

Hagel, Stefan. "Aulos." Ancient Greek Music. www.oeaw.ac.at/ kal/agm/.

————. "Cithara." Ancient Greek Music. www.oeaw.ac.at/kal/agm/.

Hammond, N. G. L. "The Speeches in Arrian's *Indica* and *Anabasis.*" *Classical Quarterly*, New Series 49, no.1 (1999): 238–253.

Jones, Ryan. "Hoplite vs. Pezhetairoi." Alexander the Great. http:// myweb.unomaha.edu/~mreames/Alexander/sarissa_jones.html.

Kern, Paul Bentley. *Ancient Siege Warfare.* Bloomington: Indiana University Press, 1999.

Lattey, Cuthbert. "The Diadochi and the Rise of King-Worship," *English Historical Review* 32, no. 127 (Jul. 1917): 321–334.

Lendering, Jona. "Alexander the Great: The 'Good' Sources." Livius: Articles on Ancient History. www.livius.org/aj-al/alexander/alexan- der_z1b.html.

————. "Arrian of Nicomedia." Livius: Articles on Ancient History. www.livius.org/arl-arz/arrian/arrian.html.

————. "Ptolemy I Soter." Livius: Articles on Ancient History. www.livius.org/ps-pz/ptolemies/ptolemy_i_soter4.html.

Leriche, Pierre. "L'extreme-orient hellenistique: Le monde de la brique crue." *Les Dossiers d'Archeologie* 179 (February 1993): 82.

Marr, John S., and Charles H. Calisher. "Alexander the Great and West Nile Virus Encephalitis." *Emerging Infectious Diseases* 9, no. 12 (Dec. 2003). wwwnc.cdc.gov/eid/article/9/12/03-0288_article. htm.

McInerney, Jeremy. "Arrian and the Greek Alexander Romance." *Classical World* 100, no. 4 (Summer 2007): 424–430.

Murison, C. L. "Darius III and the Battle of Issus." *Historia: Zeitschrift fur Alte Geschichte*, Bd. 21, H. 3 (3rd Qtr., 1972): 399–423.

Partridge, Robert. "Sacred Animals of Ancient Egypt Gallery." BBC. www.bbc.co.uk/history/ancient/egyptians/animal_gallery_12.shtml.

Peterson, Joseph H. "Avesta:Vendidad (English): Fargard 1." From *Sacred Books of the East,* American ed., 1898. Translated by James Darmesteter. www.avesta.org/vendidad/vd1sbe.htm.

Ramsay, Sir William Mitchell. *The Historical Geography of Asia Minor.* London: William Clowes and Sons, 1890.

Review of *Alexander the Great: The Death of a God,* by Paul Doherty. http://forums.civfanatics.com/archive/index.php/t-370858.html.

Rhodes, P. J. *A History of the Classical Greek World: 478–323 BC,* 2nd ed. West Sussex, UK: Wiley-Blackwell, 2010.

Robinson, C. A., Jr. "The Extraordinary Ideas of Alexander the Great." *American Historical Review* 62, no.2 (Jan. 1957): 326–344.

Sansone, David. *Ancient Greek Civilization.* Oxford: Blackwell, 2004.

Siwa Oasis. http://siwaoasis.com/.

"Thais." www.tyndalehouse.com/Egypt/ptolemies/thais_fr.htm.

Thompson, Jonathan. "Disease, Not Conflict, Ended the Reign of Alexander." *Independent on Sunday,* Aug. 16, 2005. www.alexander-stomb.com/main/deathofalexander/IoS6on7Aug05b.JPG.

Thompson, Michael. *Granicus 334 BC: Alexander's First Persian Victory.* New York: Osprey, 2007.

Tripathi, Ramashankar. *History of Ancient India.* New Delhi: Shri Jainendia, 1942.

Wace, Alan J. B. "Hellenistic Royal Portraits," *Journal of Hellenic Studies* 25 (1905): 86–104.

Wheeler, Benjamin. *Alexander the Great.* New York: G. P. Putnam's Sons, 1900.

Young, Rodney S. "The Excavations at Yassihuyuk-Gordion, 1950." *Archaeology* 3, no. 4 (Dec. 1950): 196–201.

———. "Making History at Gordium." *Archaeology* 6, no. 3 (Sept. 1953): 159–166.

Yirka, Bob. "Toxicologists Offer Possible Explanation for the Cause of Alexander the Great's Death." http://phys.org/news/2014-01-toxicologists-explanation-alexander-great-death.html.

ACKNOWLEDGMENTS

When I was young, very young, my grandmother would sit and answer my questions on any and all subjects. She had an impressive understanding of all sorts of information, and wherever she might lack knowledge, or if we simply wanted to learn more about a certain subject, we would consult her *Encyclopedia Britannica*. I remember asking her who Alexander the Great was, though I can't remember where I first heard his name. She said he was a king who conquered the world (or what he knew of it) and then died tragically young. We decided to look him up in the encyclopedia. Reading the relatively short biography was enough for me. I was hooked. It is to her this book is dedicated.

I thank my wife, Tobey, for her patience and consideration in allowing me to work on this book, and my children, Jace and Agatha, for the wonderful distraction. Thanks to Drew Preston for the great notes and encouragement. Thanks, too, to the staff of the Boone County Public Library, Kentucky, and the staff of the Steely Library at Northern Kentucky University for their help and resources. Thanks to Bruce H. Franklin of Westholme Publishing for the support and opportunity, Ron Silverman for his copy editing and recommendations, Paul Dangel for his maps, Mike Kopf for his proofreading, and Trudi Gershenov for her beautiful cover design.

INDEX

Note: In page references, m indicates maps.